THE YOUNG DECORATOR

THE YOUNG DECORATOR

A Textbook for
High Schools and a
Guide for All Home
Decorators

Phyllis Sloan Allen

Brigham Young
University Press

Courtesy of Clopoy Corporation.

Special note:
Permission is granted to
teachers to reproduce assignment
sheets and work sheets in order that
the materials in the book may
remain intact.

Library of Congress Cataloging in Publication Data

Allen, Phyllis Sloan.
The young decorator.

SUMMARY: A high school textbook introducing
basic principles and techniques of interior
decorating and furnishing.
1.   House furnishings—Juvenile literature.
2.   Interior decoration—Juvenile literature.
[1.   House furnishings.   2.   Interior decoration]
I.   Title
TX311.A43   747   74-23449
ISBN 0-8425-0654-3
ISBN 0-8425-0062-6 (pbk.)

International Standard Book Number: 0-8425-0654-3 (hardback)
                                                          0-8425-0062-6 (paperback)
Library of Congress Catalog Card Number: 74-23449
Brigham Young University Press, Provo, Utah 84602
© 1975 Brigham Young University Press. All rights reserved
Third printing 1979
Printed in the United States of America
79   15Mp   37785

Dedicated
to all young people upon
whom the quality of the
future homes
of America depends.

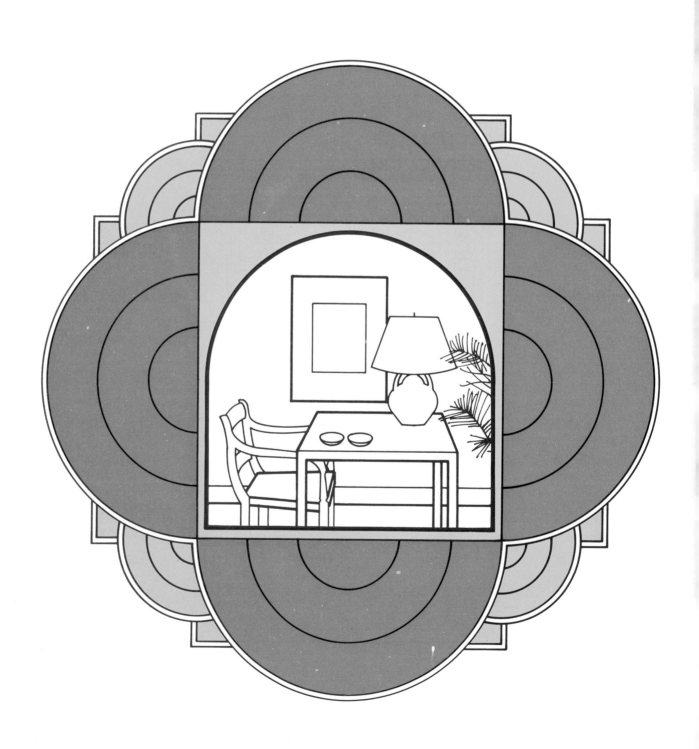

Contents

Color Illustrations   xi
Preface   xiii
Introduction   xvii

Part 1: Where to Begin   1
What are the choices in homes
  for young moderns?   3
  Conventional dwelling   3
  Apartment dwelling   4
  The condominium   4
  The mobile home   6
  Factory-built homes   7
Making space work for you   11
  *The basic requirements of a good
    floor plan*   12
  Other considerations   12
Suggested teaching aids and
  procedures   16
Student assignments   16

Part 2: Developing Good Taste   19
How to acquire good taste   21
General categories of design   22
  Structural design   22
  Decorative design   22
Principles and elements of design   23
  Principles of design   23
  Elements of design   29
Arranging furniture   33
  Guidelines   33
  Some special considerations   34
  When the room is small   40
Personalize your walls   43
Suggested teaching aids and
  procedures   47
Student assignments   47

Part 3: Your Own Color Schemes   57
Color is your most important tool;
  make it work for you   59
  Know the color wheel   59
  Color's three dimensions   61
  Color scheming   62
  *Other things you should know
    about color*   64
Suggested teaching aids and
  procedures   70
Student assignments   70

Part 4: Start with Backgrounds 77
Floors 79
Hard surface flooring 79
Nonresilient 80
Wood floors 81
Resilient 82
Choosing the right carpet: some guidelines 84
Caring for your carpet 88
Walls 89
Rigid wall coverings 89
Masonry 90
Paneling 91
Working wonders with wallpaper 90
Common terms 92
Wallpaper as problem solver 95
Suggested teaching aids and procedures 96
Student assignments 96

Part 5: Fabric Works Magic 99
Know about fibers 101
Natural fibers 101
Man-made fibers 102
Solving problems with fabric 106
Lighten a room 106
Emphasize or conceal objects or architectural features 106
Set the mood of a room 106
Make a room either masculine or feminine 106
Make a room appear larger or smaller 106
What goes with what? 108
Suggested teaching aids and procedures 110
Student assignments 110

Part 6: No Window Problems 115
Learn about windows 117
Basic types of windows 117
Window terminology 118
Types of window hangings 122

Procedure for measuring a window and estimating yardage 124
Selecting the fabric 126
Same window — different look 130
Take a tall, old-fashioned window 130
Take a nearly square window 130
Take two side-by-side windows 130
How to make your own curtains and drapery 135
Draperies unlined, lined, or both lined and interlined 135
To make pinch-pleat headings 136
Easypleat headings 138
Suggested teaching aids and procedures 140
Student assignments 140

Part 7: Fun with Furniture 145
Purchase with a plan 147
Important things to look for in wood furniture 148
Design 148
Flexibility 148
Construction 148
Use of plastic in furniture 152
Shopping tips for buying upholstered furniture 155
Furniture marketing methods 155
What about style? 156
"Fun" furniture for young moderns 156
A survey report of furniture purchases 160
Furniture care 163
Suggested teaching aids and procedures 166
Student assignments 166

Part 8: Stretching Your Dollar 169
Multipurpose furniture 171
Bargains in furniture 172

Do-it-yourself furniture 173
Treasures out of discards 176
Refinishing furniture 181
New surfaces for old with paint 184
Fabric, fabric everywhere 187
Accessories: the importance of
  little things 190
Books are like friends 192
Flowers and growing plants show
  you care 193
Take a needle and some yarn 194
More ideas from here and there 196
A formula for successful
  decoration 201
Suggested teaching aids and
  procedures 202
Student assignments 202

Part 9: Looking to the Future 205
Test your talent for decorating 207
  *Are your decisions determined by
    your lifestyle?* 207
  *What about arrangement and
    organization of space?* 207
  *Can you make color work for
    you?* 208
  *Have you discovered the magic
    of fabric?* 208
  How practical are you? 208
  *Do you recognize the importance
    of little things?* 208
  *Have you cultivated
    self-discipline?* 209
  How perceptive are you? 209
What is an interior designer? 209
  *What are the functions of an interior
    designer?* 209
  What training is necessary? 210
  *Career opportunities in interior
    design* 210
A word to young marrieds 211
Bibliography 215
  Index 217

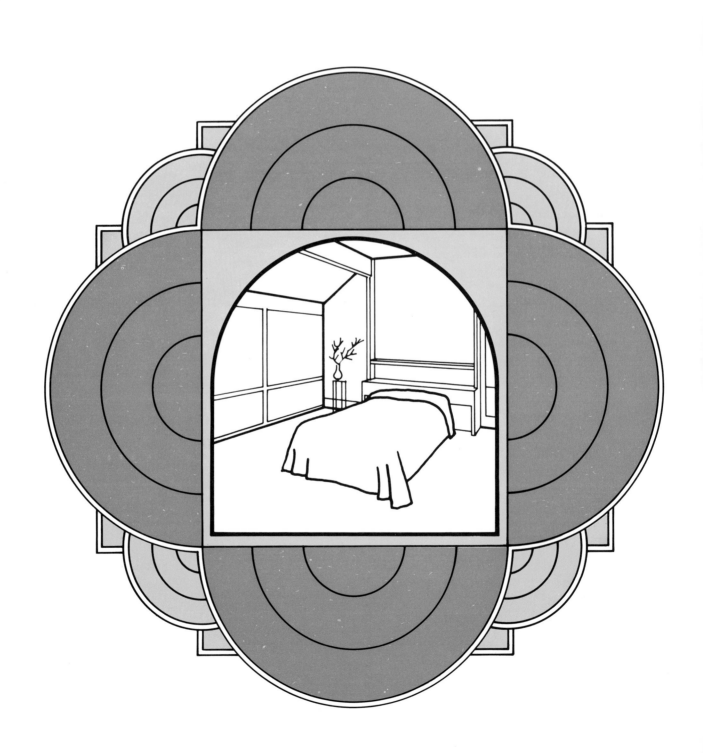

Color Illustrations

frontispiece   ii

Colorplates
1. Fireside comfort   xix
2. Conversation area   xx
3. Planning a family room   17
4. Creating a corner   18
5. Creativity in a one-room apartment   35
6. A storage wall   36
7. Color schemes   37
   Early-American: a timeless look   37
8. Room for two   38
9. One-color scheming   56
10. Color wheel   65
11. Planning color transition   66
12. Using color to create a mood   75
13. Start with . . . a white background   76
14. Avoid stereotyping: washable vinyl   93
   A playroom for any age   93
15. A unique bathroom design   94
16. Start with . . . an area rug   97

17. The magic of fabric   98
18. Create a mood: coordinated fabrics   113
19. Window nook   114
20. Framing a garden   131
21. Coordination: to unify a room   132
22. Window placement   143
23. Furniture fun   144
24. A do-it-yourself room   167
25. An attic room: eclectic   168
26. A boy's room   185
27. A basement room   186
28. Color and imagination create a room   203
29. The lived-in look   204

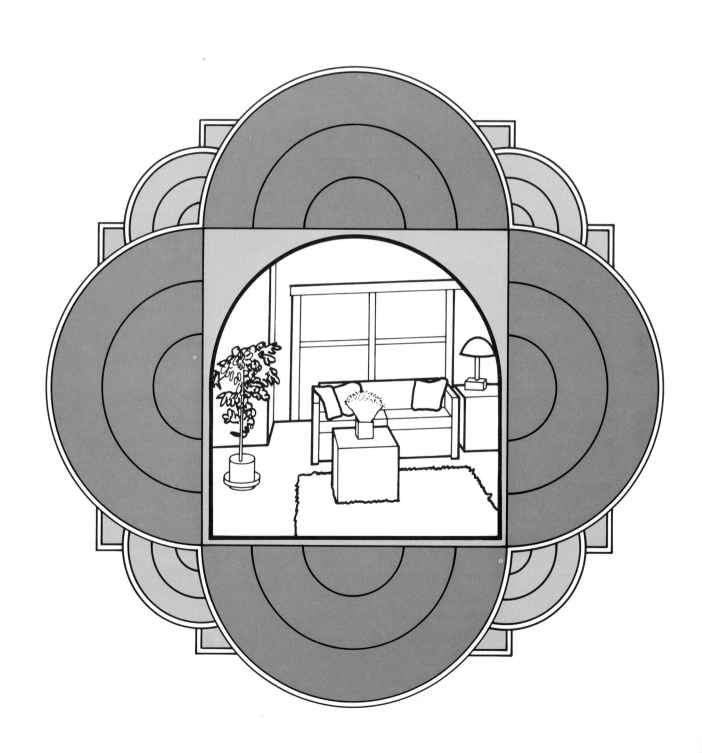

Preface

The *Young Decorator* is written on the assumption that every young person dreams of having, at some future time, a home of his own. Since the environment created in one's home is an outgrowth of established values of beauty and efficiency, it is important that these values be based upon basic design principles and guidelines. It is the purpose of this book to assist you, through the knowledge and the application of these principles and guidelines, to develop not only a sensitivity to good design but a discriminating taste upon which to establish lasting values. To accomplish this, *The Young Decorator* presents a practical approach to help you solve design problems relating to your own circumstances.

When you open the door to welcome friends into your home, the view that greets them is a reflection of you. It reveals, through the things you have chosen and how you have put them together, either a discriminating taste or a lack of taste. *Neither is dependent upon the amount of money spent.*

Probably the most important ingredients of a home are individuality and warmth. To achieve these, avoid being influenced by each fad or fashion that comes along or copying what someone else has done. Rather, strive to create for you and your family an environment that is appropriate to your own life style. To get the best value for your money, look for furnishings that honestly fit the way you live. In this process, you will run into a variety of problems and will need answers to many questions. To seek outside help is only prudent, but total reliance upon the decisions of others in matters of planning and decorating for your family is unwise. You know more about your needs than anyone else; the final decision should be yours.

The big market in home furnishings today is for the budget-minded young married group. Never before has the choice in furnishings been so wide nor have options been so varied. But the more options you have, the more carefully you must discriminate before making a long-term purchase. Unfortunately, the percentage of inferior household furnishings available today is far too high. The aim of this book is to assist you in discriminating between what is good and what is not good design and to help you in making each major purchase for your home an investment in appropriateness and excellence that will give you enduring satisfaction.

I hope that every young person will be sufficiently motivated to study and search for satisfactory solutions to his own decorating problems in order to create a home with character and individuality, keeping in mind that charm and beauty have no price tag.

The Young Decorator is divided into nine major units. At the end of each unit are suggestions to teachers concerning illustrative materials, guest speakers, field trips, and student assignments.

Ten work sheets with objectives, working materials, and instructions to students are included. These are provided to give the student practical exercises in applying the lesson material.

Part one, "Where to Begin," first surveys the choices of various types of dwellings available to young people today, discussing the advantages and disadvantages of each, after which it focuses on planning or choosing an efficient floor plan.

Part two, "Developing Good Taste," is concerned with making the reader aware of what constitutes good taste and of how it can be developed. Principles and guidelines given in the lesson can be applied by making liveable and functional arrangements and artistic wall compositions.

Part three, "Your Own Color Schemes," examines color as the most important and least costly of all decorating tools.

Part four, "Start with Backgrounds," explores the boom in hard-surface flooring, the unprecedented growth in the carpet industry, and the wonders that can be accomplished with today's wall coverings.

Part five, "Fabric Works Magic," concentrates on the use of fabric as the key to successful decoration.

Part six, "No Window Problems," deals with exciting challenges in decorating windows. It gives practical information on measuring and estimating yardage, and provides a step-by-step procedure in making pleated drapery.

Part seven, "Fun with Furniture," focuses on important things to look for when one is shopping for furniture and offers information on how to care for it.

Part eight, "Stretching Your Dollar," suggests numerous things one can do on a tiny budget to create a home with character. The importance of little things is emphasized.

Part nine, "Looking to the Future," includes a questionnaire that will test your talent for decorating. The definition of an interior designer is given, and the functions of and the necessary training and career opportunities for the interior designer are explained.

The book concludes with a word to young marrieds, offering useful guidelines which, if followed, will turn a house into a place to be lived in and used, a place to be enjoyed — a home.

Introduction

Home. When you hear that word, what does it mean to you? Does it mean a place where love is — a place for fun? Or does it mean merely a place to eat and sleep — or even to run from? In "Death of the Hired Man" Robert Frost says, "home is the place where, when you have to go there, they have to take you in." But to most people home is the place that is a refuge where we find love, security, and comfort, where we get daily reassurance in seeing familiar things such as the same rooms, furniture, paintings, books, and personal belongings.

Home is where each of us develops his individuality. It is where we learn to eat, to speak, to dress, and to relate to other people. Home is where we learn to do some of the important tasks of living and where we do what we *want* to do when we don't *have* to do anything. Home is where we acquire the culture that makes us what we are; where we expand to our full growth and capability through day-to-day living.

A home should be a place where interests and values are established and goals are developed; where children learn to appreciate good books, music, and art, and where one learns respect and love for others. There is real value in a well-designed physical environment. It can help set the proper emotional climate for children to grow in and for adults to live in comfortably. Through day-to-day observation of our surroundings, tastes, values, and attitudes that carry through our entire lives are established. The preferences of young people, their appreciation or lack of appreciation of quality and good design, are outgrowths of the environment in which their taste develops.

Environmental scientists emphasize the importance of the environment upon the formation of attitudes and character development during the formative years. What can young parents do today to build in their children an awareness and an appreciation of good taste? Perhaps a planned program beginning with the physical home environment in which the characteristics they wish to develop are an integral part would be the most positive approach.

Good decorating is made up of many factors: taste, value, style, individuality, comfort, and convenience. It is the art of creating a personal environment shaped with tangible elements through the application of intangible principles. A successful room does not just happen. No matter how easy-going or casual it may look, it will show evidence of basic design principles and will always be attuned to the life-style of the occupant.

The key to successful decorating is suitability. By surrounding yourself with the things that are suitable to your way of life, you express your own taste. Whether or not taste is good depends upon the ingredients you choose and the manner in which you blend them. The measure of success or failure in decorating one's home is not dependent upon the amount of money spent but rather upon how those who live there feel about it. It is possible to create what may be a decorator's dream house that will be a failure as a real home. If you develop a meaningful environment for you and your family, one in which all who live there feel comfortable, you will have created a framework within which to nurture good taste and an appreciation of quality and beauty.

Where to Begin

COLORPLATE 2. An inviting conversation area is created with clean-lined furniture covered with washable corduroy, a simple wall shelf that serves a myriad of uses, and scrubbable vinyl wall covering that adds height and sets the room's color scheme. Lively colors have a youth appeal. *Courtesy of Imperial and Collins and Aikman.*

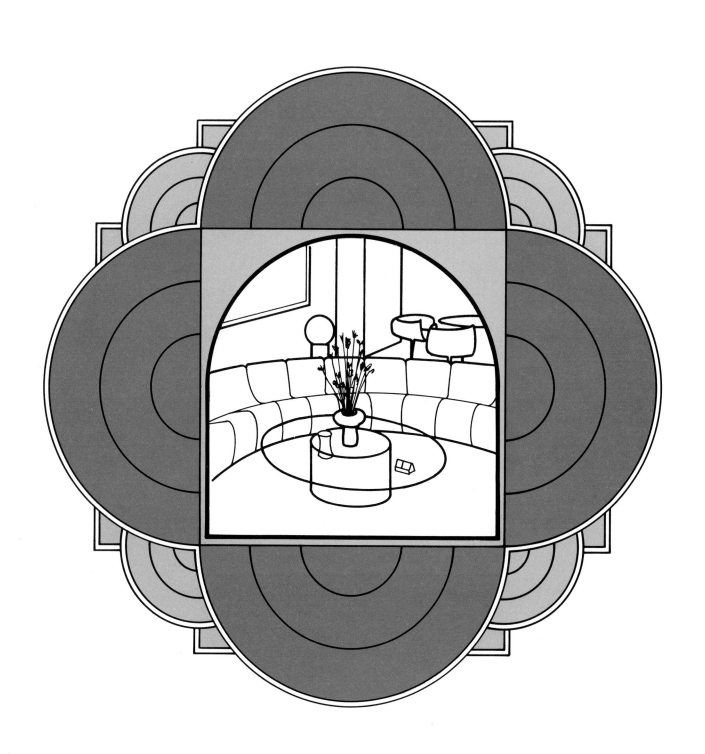

Many centuries ago man first began to gather raw materials and put them together to make shelters against the weather and the ravaging of beasts. Since that time, various architectural styles have evolved. The enduring styles have developed gradually and naturally through the use of available materials and facilities to fill the basic needs and to express the individual characteristics of people living under particular circumstances.

Since those early days, the American home has been the great pride of most of our citizens. Today 75 percent of the American people prefer a single family dwelling. In no other country in the world do so many people live in homes of their own nor do they have so many comforts and conveniences as in America.

The dream of most young people is to have a home of their own; but too often they expect to begin their married lives in a living situation equivalent to that for which their parents worked, planned, and saved many years to acquire. With today's soaring prices, starting out with a fully equipped home is becoming unrealistic. Where, then, do young couples begin?

What are the Choices in Homes for Young Moderns?

Conventional Dwelling

The few who are financially able to buy a home when they begin married life may choose from a great variety of styles. But before entering upon such a venture as purchasing a home, they should carefully investigate all of the financial details involved and be aware of the liabilities and pitfalls as well as the advantages.

Buying a home will likely be the largest purchase you will ever make. Seek the advice of people who are knowledgeable in the field and whom you respect. When a home purchase

3

seems feasible, study styles of domestic architecture to determine which style is the right one for you. Your particular life-style should be the criterion upon which the choice is made, not the trend of the moment or the persuasiveness of a real estate man.

After much careful study and deliberation, ask yourselves many questions to determine your own likes and dislikes: Do you favor a traditional house or a modern one? Which suits your personality and life-style? What about resale value? When the decision to buy has been made, put your most conscientious efforts into creating the "home of your dreams" and into taking pleasure in the pride of ownership. Nothing you do will be more rewarding than establishing a home and a family to enjoy it.

Apartment Dwelling

A second alternative in choosing your first "home" is an apartment. Here you pay a monthly rent with utilities and laundry costs added. There are no obligations outside of the apartment itself, and privacy is usually one of the advantages for single people or for a couple. But apartment living, if you have children, is usually not desirable, and many apartment houses do not allow children. However, for the first year of establishing a home the apartment often is the most readily available and most economical type of housing.

The Condominium

Another alternative in the choice of a home is the condominium. *Condominium* is actually a Latin word dating back to the sixth century, meaning *joint dominium* or *joint ownership*. In the present sense, it is a cooperative ven-

4

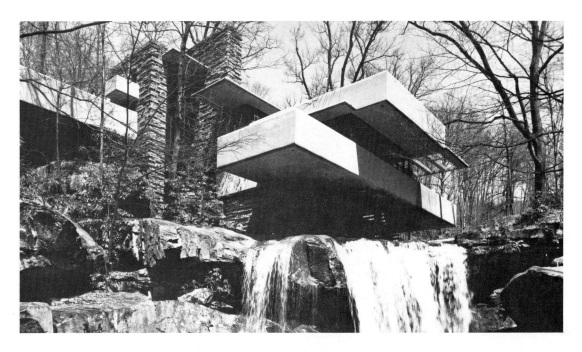

(Far left). A well-designed traditional home is never outdated. *Courtesy of Capital Industries.* (Above). Good modern design will become classic as this home called Falling Water, built in 1936 at Bear Run, Pennsylvania, and designed by Frank Lloyd Wright. *Courtesy of Western Pennsylvania Conservancy; photo by Michael Tedison.* **(Below).** Privacy and ownership without maintenance worries make condomium living popular with young and old.

5

The mobile home can be neat and comfortable and easily moved. It is playing a role of increased importance.

ture. The occupant is the sole owner of his own apartment or house in a multifamily project but shares common areas and elements of the property such as gardens, swimming pools, and lobbies with other co-owners. All owners share in making the rules governing the project, and in many places they also share in assuming the responsibility of enforcing the rules.

Once thought of as a place for a weekend retreat, condominium living is booming. Many refinements have been added, and today condominiums have become year-round dwellings for many families. The big plus seems to be no maintenance worries. All mechanical conveniences that contribute to creature comforts, such as utility centers, electrical apparatus, heating, and air conditioning are taken care of. There are, however, some minuses. There is no place to putter outside nor enough storage for "pack rats"; one must work with neighbors over common problems that arise, and present costs are high.

The Mobile Home

Still another alternative in housing is the mobile home — the oldest form of industrialized housing. When they were first put on the market, mobile homes were looked upon as the poor relations of housing, and the mobile home parks were a dreaded neighborhood liability. Today they are playing a role of increased importance. Radical changes have taken place in the homes themselves and in the minds of most people regarding them. With the skyrocketing prices, the need for "manu-

6

factured housing'' has increased, the greatest demand coming from the young and the old. In 1972 the largest number of mobile homes was purchased by people under thirty-three and over fifty-five years of age. With the present increase in the number of people between twenty and thirty-four and fifty-five and seventy-four, the demand is increasing dramatically.

The name *mobile home* is a misnomer since these homes spend only 1 percent of their time on the move. They began in the housing shortage days of the 1940s when they provided makeshift shelter. The Mobile Home Manufacturers Association calls a mobile home a ''transportable structure built on a chassis and designed to be used as a dwelling unit with or without a permanent foundation when connected with the required utilities.'' The average size is 12' wide, 60' long, and 12' high. Some are larger, and some are made in two or more parts that may be separated, towed separately, and put together horizontally. They are complete with living room, dining area, kitchen, utility room, bathroom (one, one and one-half, or two baths), and one to three bedrooms. Wall paneling, carpeting, draperies, and many built-ins are furnished.

The past concern that ''mobile towns'' are harmful to the aesthetic environment is becoming less of a problem. Future mobile home subdivisions promise to be better planned and surrounded by gardens that may be owned and maintained by the occupants.

The public in general today is becoming better informed on housing at all levels. A growing awareness of and a demand for better quality and design in all housing are bringing about improvements in the mobile home. Evidence of this is seen not only in the recent alliance between industry and architecture but also in an increased sophistication in technology and in a growing belief that good design need not be costly. In the last decade the price per square foot of mobile homes has actually declined, while the cost of conventional housing has soared.

One of the challenges to every homemaker living in a mobile home or a tract development of any kind is to give that home an atmosphere that is unique to her particular family — a feeling of individuality. Individuality is an elusive quality, particularly in a house. It develops slowly and naturally with the personality of the family. In custom-built homes this development is not too difficult, but in subdivisions, where house after house is the same, it is a real challenge for each owner to give to his or her dwelling that personal mark.

Factory-built Homes

Still another alternative for low-cost housing is the factory-built home. Today's market for new homes far exceeds the available supply, and conventional construction cannot keep pace with present-day demands. Something must be done. Some method must be adopted to produce homes for young people inexpensively and fast.

7

So why not factory-built homes? Already they are purchased and enjoyed by many people, and some industry sources predict that soon half of the nation's housing will be produced at the factory.

Factory-built houses come in three basic types: (1) the prefabricated house which consists of various components put together at the factory and shipped to the site for immediate assembling; (2) the pre-cut house in which all materials are cut, sized, and labeled in sequence for fast erection; and (3) the modular house which is put together and shipped in two or more units to be joined at the site to form a complete dwelling.

A number of benefits derive from buying these houses. Because factory-produced homes are built in quantity, (1) there is less waste, (2) quality can be controlled, and (3) inspection is done at less cost, which adds up to better homes for less money. Another item to be considered here is time. Often people take months and even years to decide to buy a home, but when the decision is made, they want instant results. The conventional route to building is subject to many uncertainties and hazards. Scarcity of available skilled labor, vandalism, and pilferage of materials may all contribute to delay and unexpected expense.

The factory-built house is not a new concept, but in the past some valid objections to it have arisen. Too often

8

(Far left, above). Wood frame modules, bolted to steel carriers, are delivered to site by truck. *Courtesy of Hudson Houses Inc.* (Far left, below). House is erected by a three-man crew in less than eight hours. Room modules are rolled across foundation on aluminum tracks. *Courtesy of Hudson Houses Inc.* (Above). Modules are bolted together. Flashing is secured; wall intersections are trimmed out. The house is ready for occupancy. *Courtesy of Hudson Houses Inc.* (Below). Privacy, comfort, and pride of ownership at a minimum of cost. Ready for living. *Courtesy of Hudson Houses Inc.*

9

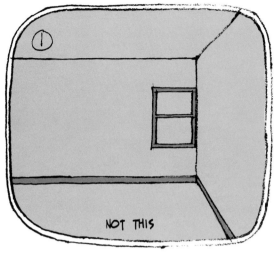

NOT THIS

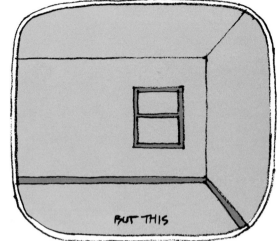

BUT THIS

it has been thought of as a house completely lacking in character, to be purchased only as the last resort. This public resistance is rapidly changing because of the improvement in design and construction and the high cost of traditional building methods.

Another stumbling block to the purchase of an assembly line house has been the variance in the rules of local building codes. With the hope of developing a national market for industrialized housing, measures are being taken in many states to establish through legislation state-wide building standards. Should these standards be adopted throughout the country, factories could operate at peak efficiency with a high degree of standardization of design, materials, and price and could thus provide good quality low-cost housing in quantity to meet the demand.

During the 1950s and 1960s, tract developments presented neighborhoods where row upon row of look-alike houses presented an atmosphere

of total anonymity. Individual families were hard put to give to their homes a feeling of personality in a maze of sameness. This trend is being reversed today. In more and more planned communities, houses of varying styles are clustered in such a way as to take advantage of natural surroundings and to create a feeling of individual living. Price will remain somewhat lower than in custom-built dwellings, and this is a major consideration. But because of the cooperative nature of the communities, proximity can lead to friction that will need to be resolved.

In looking to the future, planning habitations for the betterment of human life presents a constant challenge to the architect and the entire building industry. Legislation that now sets up many barriers to industrialized housing will likely be removed because of the increased pressure from greater num-

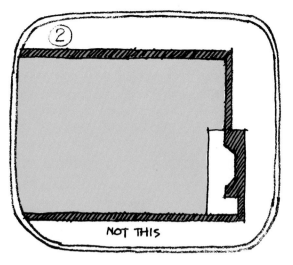

NOT THIS

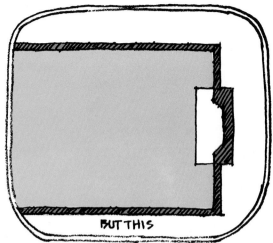

BUT THIS

bers of people. Young people searching for housing they can enjoy and afford have every reason to be optimistic about the future.

Making Space Work for You

More people will see your house from the outside than from the inside. But the inside is where you and your family are going to live. Which is more important: to present to the public a facade that may catch the eye or to have well-planned space enclosed by a simple but well-designed exterior? It does not necessarily have to be one or the other, but too often the plan begins with the outside, and space inside has to be accommodated to it. As a result, many times windows butt up against walls (1), wall space is not right for furniture, the fireplace is pushed to a corner (2), or there are too many changes of levels requiring hazardous steps between rooms. Most serious of all is that there is frequently not enough space for

living because the money was used up in an irregular multilevel facade.

The importance of well-arranged floor space cannot be overemphasized. To have a home in which the many activities of today's families can be carried on with a minimum of frustration should be the major concern of every homemaker. Even on a limited budget, if you are willing to forego expensive frills, you very likely can have the valuable space you need. It costs no more to build a house with a good plan than one with a poor plan, and it may cost much less.

There are always individual differences in the manner of living that must be considered, but experience has shown that some basic things in the general plan of a house are conducive to the smooth working of a *family home.* If young people are aware of these requirements and use them as guidelines when looking for or planning a home, they will be more likely to have efficient homes, whether they be mobile units or custom-built. If

11

enough people would know what they want and demand it, architects and builders would comply.

The Basic Requirements of a Good Floor Plan

Listed below are the requirements basic to an efficient floor plan. Look for them when buying and insist upon them when planning a house.

Well-defined basic areas

- Working and hobbies. These are the areas for cooking, washing dishes, laundering, ironing, sewing, and hobbies. They should be conveniently located with well-arranged and adequately lighted space.
- Eating areas. Space planned for quick snacks and informal family meals should be conveniently located in or near the kitchen. Where space permits more formal dining, the area should be private or should be provided with means of shutting off the eating area from the clutter of the kitchen and from the front door.
- Living, entertainment, and recreation areas. Informal: family and recreation rooms should be convenient to the kitchen and to the outside. More formal (where space is available): should be out of major traffic lanes, designed for privacy and relaxation.
- Sleeping and dressing areas should be located for quiet and privacy with good access to bathrooms.

Traffic lanes adequate but not wasteful

- Central entrance hall, channeling traffic to all areas of the house. This need not be large.
- Easy access from kitchen to front door, back door, utility room, service area, garage, and all areas of the house.
- Direct access from the utility area to the outside service area.
- Easy access from at least one living area to the outside living area.
- An access door from the front of the house directly to the kitchen, thus eliminating the necessity of always opening heavy garage doors.
- All major traffic lanes routed to avoid going through any room to reach another (the possible exception is the family room).

Well-placed openings

- Doors should be conveniently located and windows placed for easy draping.

Adequate wall space

- Space should be planned for large and necessary pieces of furniture.

Ample storage

- Storage space should be conveniently located throughout the house and in the garage.

Other Considerations

- Plumbing should be economically located wherever possible, such as between the kitchen and the utility room, between bathrooms, or in a second story directly above plumbing on the ground floor. Where possible, there should be a wash basin and a toilet near the back door.
- The fireplace should be away from the line of traffic and situated for the

(Left). Even a small apartment can have extra guest space with a sleeping bag. Wood blocks support a single spring or a door. Desk pigeonholes are also made from 6″ × 16″ pieces of wood. *Courtesy of Celanese Fibers Marketing Company.* (Above). Plan a place for muddy boots and wet coats. A handy bulletin board for messages and creative talent is a must. *Courtesy of Armstrong Cork Company.*

grouping of a private conversation area.
■ There should be a place for study. (Frequently, with a minimum of planning, available space can be used for a variety of activities. For example, the dining area may be a study or a workroom between meals. Bedrooms, if equipped with desk and light, can serve as a study and a place to work at hobbies.)

All of the rooms mentioned above will not likely be in your first home, but if you have a future plan in mind, you can work toward this goal. If you build, plan for future additions. Have the finished plan drawn and start with a portion of it. When the time comes to add a room or a wing, the cost will be less and the addition will fit naturally onto the original structure.

This is also a great help in selling a house. A prospective buyer can be shown specifically how an addition can be accomplished with the smallest number of structural changes and the least expense.

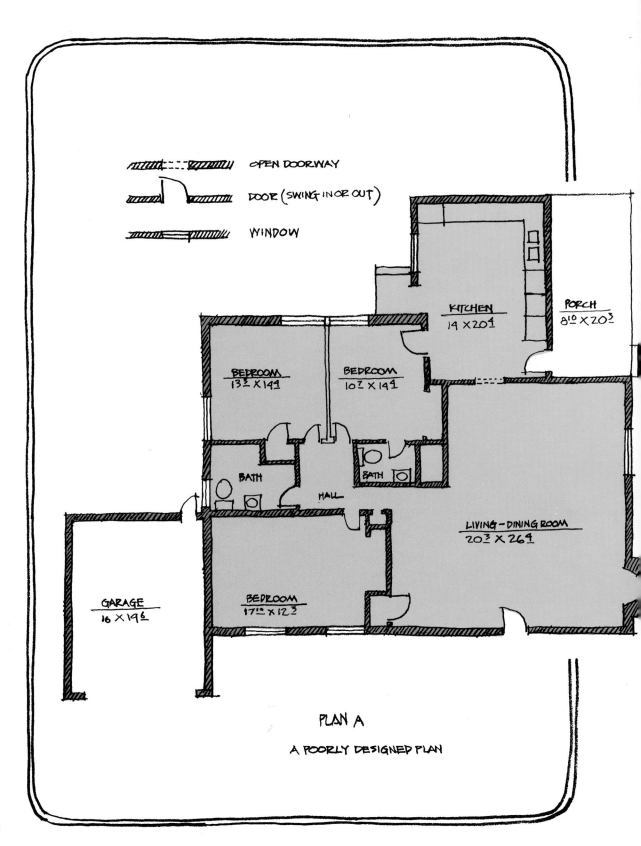

OPEN DOORWAY

DOOR (SWING IN OR OUT)

WINDOW

KITCHEN
14 X 20⁴

PORCH
8¹⁰ X 20³

BEDROOM
13³ X 14⁴

BEDROOM
10³ X 14⁴

BATH

BATH

HALL

LIVING - DINING ROOM
20³ X 26⁴

GARAGE
16 X 19⁶

BEDROOM
17¹⁰ X 12³

PLAN A

A POORLY DESIGNED PLAN

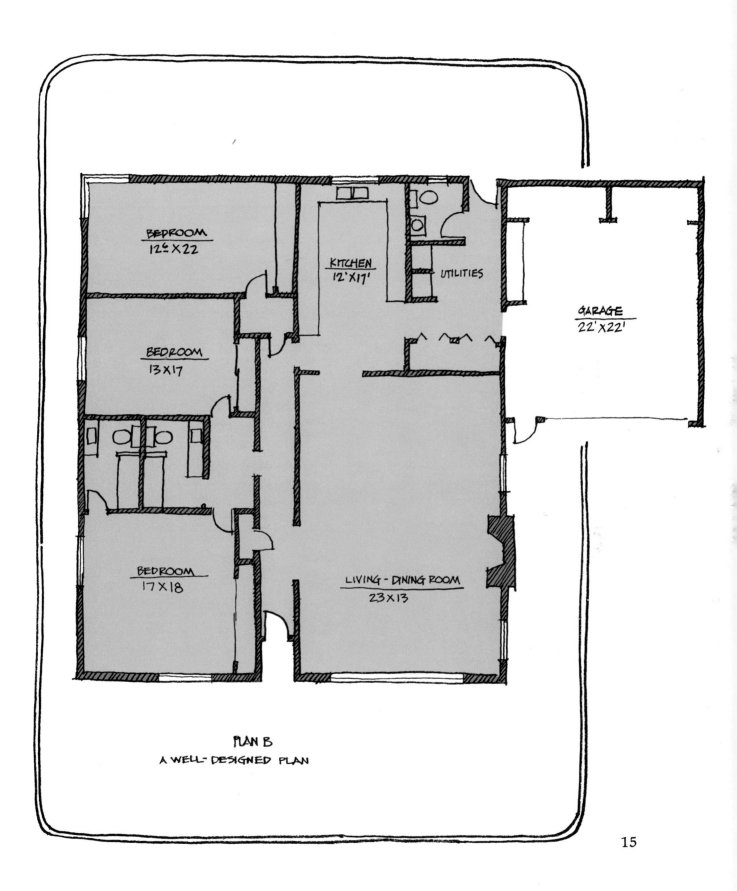

BEDROOM
12⁶ X 22

KITCHEN
12' X 17'

UTILITIES

GARAGE
22' X 22'

BEDROOM
13 X 17

BEDROOM
17 X 18

LIVING - DINING ROOM
23 X 13

PLAN B
A WELL-DESIGNED PLAN

15

Suggestions and Assignments for Part One: Where to Begin

Suggested Teaching Aids and Procedures

1.   Encourage discussion and response from students.
2.   Get information and illustrations of the various types of dwellings discussed in the introduction.
3.   Bring in an outside speaker: a business man who plans, constructs, or sells low-cost housing.
4.   Invite a member of the city commission to talk to students about the problems and future prospects of mobile housing units or factory-built homes in your area.
5.   Take students on a field trip to explore some of these types of homes in your community.
6.   Discuss each of the requirements of a good floor plan.
7.   Show illustrations of both good and bad floor plans.

8.   Take students on a field trip to see a house under construction where the walls are up but with no interior finishing. Point out the good and bad features in the floor plan as well as the placement of doors and windows.

Student Assignments

1.   Make inquiries to get information concerning the pros and cons of the types of dwellings discussed.
2.   Study written material and sketches in the text.
3.   Make a sketch of your own floor plan at home. Point out the good and bad features. Suggest how the plan could be improved.
4.   Observe floor plans in magazines. Check each one carefully to reinforce your awareness of what is good and what is not good planning.

The assignments and work sheets in this book may be reproduced. (See special note on the copyright page of this book.)

COLORPLATE 3. Good taste begins with a plan. Here a room for snacks, games, and conversation is well-arranged and uncluttered yet serves a variety of needs. Cool and warm colors combine to create a pleasant mood. *Courtesy of Syroco.*

2

Developing Good Taste

COLORPLATE 4. A corner for comfort. A wicker sofa is covered with double-knit slip covers, an old quilt becomes a table cover, and a collection of prints and painting make a personal wall arrangement. *Courtesy of Celanese Corporation.*

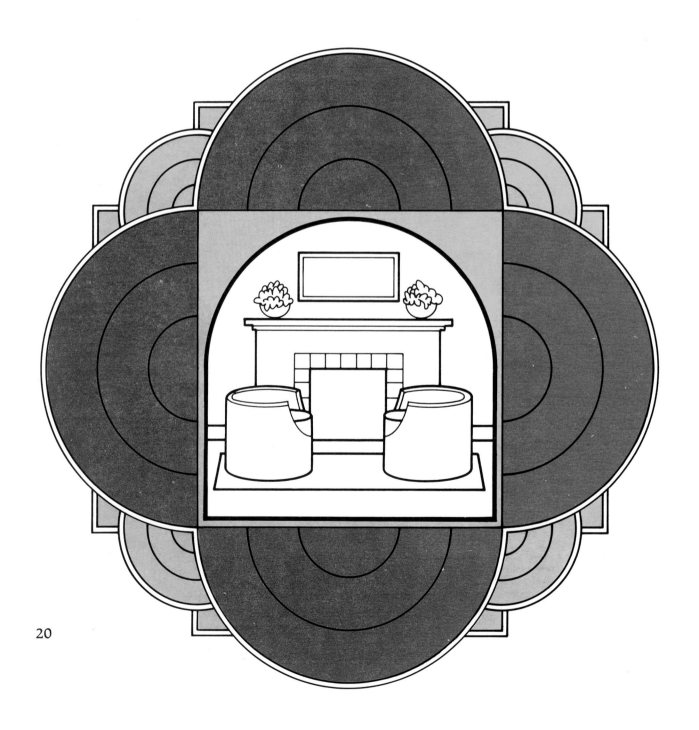

What are the ingredients that make up a well-designed room? How can a novice judge what is good and what is not good design, and how can one go about achieving good taste? One is not born with good taste. Taste is not acquired by accepting each new trend that comes along, but rather through a deliberate and continuing process of first becoming "aware," then training the eye to discriminate between what is good and what is not good design. It is a matter of weighing, sifting, and considering. If one is seriously interested in developing good taste, it can be done by following the guidelines listed below.

How to Acquire Good Taste

1. First of all, acquire a knowledge of the principles and elements of design, and how each plays an important part in the planning of a room.
2. Then deliberately apply these principles until design which has been recognized over the years as "good" becomes good to you.
3. Develop the habit of careful and constant observation. Wherever you go, notice light and shadow, shape and texture, pattern and color — not just a color in itself, but what colors do to each other. Look for balance, scale and proportion, rhythm, and emphasis. See and feel these in nature and sense the harmony which they produce. Carefully examine rooms that appeal to you. See how the principles of design have been applied.
4. Become knowledgeable about interiors of historical and contemporary styles through study and research, by regularly examining periodical magazines, and by visiting furniture stores and decorating studios. Ask questions. Look, look, and look again.
5. Learn about accessories. Become knowledgeable about the small items that are appropriate for each style of

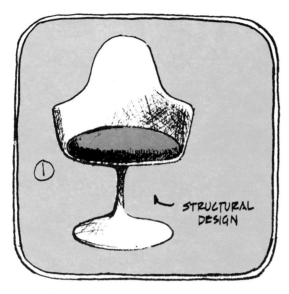

furniture, and how you can use these to enhance your rooms.

6. Remember that fashion is not a good criterion of design. As with clothes, fashion in home furnishings may soon be outdated. It is important, therefore, that you learn to be discriminating in your purchases. Whether you are buying a dish, a chair, or a house, keep in mind that *good taste is not determined by cost*. Ultimately, taste is a sense of what is appropriate to your way of life. By surrounding yourself with the things that are suitable to your pattern of living, you express your own taste. The success of your decorating depends not upon the expense or the elaborate design involved but upon the way in which you blend the ingredients that have been chosen with your home and family in mind.

General Categories of Design

Design falls into two general categories: structural and decorative.

Structural Design

Structural design relates to the size and shape of an object wherein the design is an integral part of the structure itself. For example, modern architecture both inside and out frankly reveals the materials which make up the basic structure. The design of a piece of modern furniture is seen in the form itself (1).

Decorative Design

Decorative design relates to the ornamentation of the basic structure which may be achieved through the selection and placement of color, line, and texture (2). Decorative design falls into three classifications:

- Naturalistic, realistic, or photographic, in which the motif is reproduced from nature in its natural form.
- Conventional or stylistic, in which the motif is taken from nature but is adapted to suit the shape or purpose of the object to be decorated.
- Abstract, in which nature is not necessarily the source; and, in cases where it is, the source is not clearly visible, such as plaids, stripes, checks, and strapwork (3).

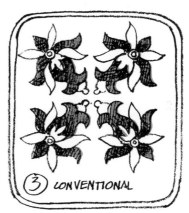

Principles and Elements of Design

A knowledge of the principles and elements of design is basic to the development of good taste.

Principles of Design

Design principles can point the way to successful decorating if one becomes knowledgeable about these principles and how to apply them. They are: scale and proportion, balance, rhythm, emphasis, and harmony.

Scale and Proportion

Scale refers to the overall size of an object or to its parts compared to other objects, regardless of shape. This must begin with the house itself and must include all the elements involved. To cite some examples: all architectural features must be in the correct scale for the house; furniture ought to be in the proper scale for the room; a lamp ought not to be too large nor too small for the

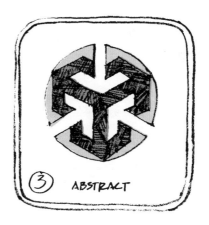

23

table it stands on (4), and the lamp shade must be in the proper scale for the base (5).

Proportion involves shape and encompasses the relationship of one part of an object to other parts, or to the whole, and the relationship of one object to another (6).

It was the Greeks who discovered the secret of good proportion and set down rules we still follow today. Their standard of good proportion is the golden rectangle with its sides in the ratio, two parts to three (7). Other pleasant relationships are 3:5, 4:7, or 5:8. By multiplying any of these combinations of figures, you can plan larger proportions when planning the dimensions of a room or selecting a piece of furniture for a particular area. For example, you have a wall space 8'; the best length for a case piece such as a stereo would be 5' (8). The Greeks also discovered that the division of a line somewhere between one half and one third its length is the most pleasing. This is called the *golden mean* (9). There are many places in which the golden mean can be applied, such as in hanging pictures and tying back drapery. It should become an unconscious part of your decorating skill.

Balance

Balance is that quality in a room that gives a sense of equilibrium and repose. There are three types of balance: formal, or *bisymmetrical* balance, in which identical objects are arranged similarly on either side of an imaginary line; informal, or *asymmetrical* balance, in which objects of differing sizes, shapes, and colors are used in an infinite number of ways to create a feeling of equilibrium (for example, a small object moved out will balance a large object up close [a principle much

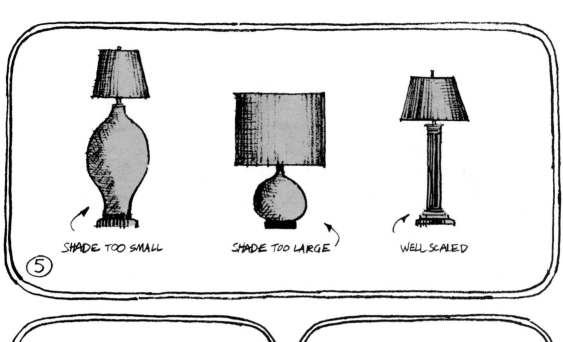

⑤ SHADE TOO SMALL   SHADE TOO LARGE   WELL SCALED

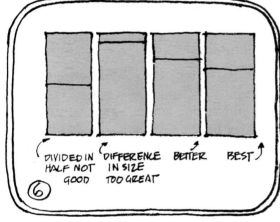

⑥ DIVIDED IN HALF NOT GOOD   DIFFERENCE IN SIZE TOO GREAT   BETTER   BEST

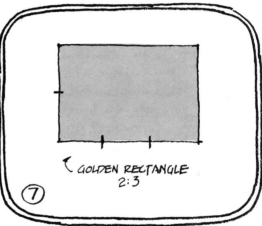

⑦ GOLDEN RECTANGLE 2:3

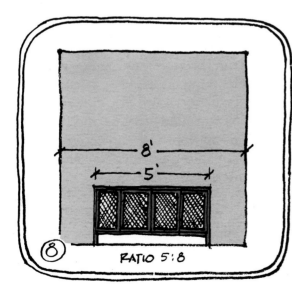

⑧ 8'   5'   RATIO 5:8

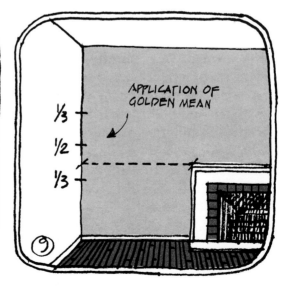

⑨ ⅓   ½   ⅓   APPLICATION OF GOLDEN MEAN

25

BISYMMETRICAL   ASYMMETRICAL   RADIAL

⑩

like the teeter-totter], and a little bit of
bright color will balance a larger area
of dull color); and *radial balance*, in
which all elements of a design radiate
from a central point, seen in the arms of
a chandelier or where chairs surround a
table. Most rooms have both formal
and informal balance; radial balance
may not always be present (10).

Rhythm

Rhythm assists the eye in moving easily
about the room and may be achieved
in five ways: by *repetition*, in which
identical objects, colors, or fabrics are
repeated; by *gradation*, in which a color
gradates from light to dark or objects
gradate from large to small; by
opposition, where two lines meet at
right angles; by *transition*, where
rhythm is found in a curved line, and
by *radiation*, in which lines radiate
from a central axis (11).

All five of these methods may not
necessarily be present in a single room.

Emphasis

Emphasis in a room is its focal point.
In every well-planned room there
should be one feature that is dominant.
It may be the fireplace, a picture
window, a striking piece of furniture,
or a storage wall. Whatever it is, make
it important (12).

Harmony

Harmony, or *unity*, is essential in any
well-designed room. A unifying theme
must run through the component parts
and blend them together. The furniture
must be compatible with the architectural background. Colors and fabrics
must be appropriate, and accessories
must enhance the larger elements and
add interest. If you want a casual look,
choose textured fabrics, gay colors, and
natural woods. If you prefer a formal
look, choose more refined fabric, more
neutralized colors, and finely grained
woods. Never follow a theme too

26

27

THE FIREPLACE IS THE FOCAL POINT
OR EMPHASIS

TOO MUCH PATTERN

TOO STARK

WELL PLANNED

slavishly but strive to maintain a
general feeling of unity throughout.

Elements of Design

Elements of design are your decorating
tools. They are: texture, pattern,
line, form, space, color, and light.

Texture

Texture refers to the surface quality of
objects and adds much to visual
interest. In general, rough textures will
create an informal atmosphere, while
smooth and shiny textures give a more
formal feeling.

Pattern

Pattern is the simplest way of desig-
nating surface enrichment. Too much
pattern can make a room too busy and
uncomfortable, while a room devoid of
pattern may be too stark and lacking in
character (13).

Line

Line is important in establishing the
feeling of the room and can seemingly
alter the proportion of an object or of
an entire room. Two identical rectangles appear to be changed when
one is divided by a horizontal line
and the other by a vertical line.
The vertical line directs the eye
across the area making it appear
wider (14). Each kind of line pro-
duces its particular psychological
effect upon a room. Vertical lines tend
to give height, strength, and dignity.
Horizontal lines tend to create feelings
of repose, solidity, and masculinity.
Diagonal lines produce a feeling of

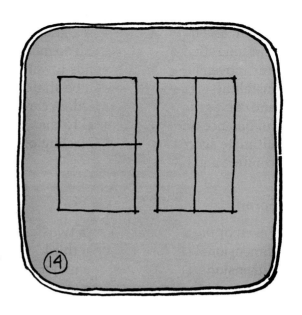

29

action, and curved lines have a graceful feminine effect upon a room. Too much line movement in a room tends toward instability. Furniture should be static, and curves should be restrained. A careful balance of line is essential to the ultimate success of a room's feeling of comfort and harmony.

Form

Form, or *mass*, occurs when a two-dimensional shape takes on a third dimension. This element is a major concern in the planning of interiors, wherein we perceive form as objects of furniture that require space and that may be moved to various locations. It must be kept in mind that too much variety in form may produce a room with a feeling of confusion, while a lack of variety may result in monotony. Form within a room is discussed in the furniture arrangement section.

Space

Space is probably the most important element of domestic architecture. Well-planned and well-organized space makes for a smooth-working home. Pleasant rooms, free of clutter, with an occasional empty corner will aid in producing that highly desirable feeling of tranquility. The arrangement of space in a house is discussed under floor plans in part one.

Color

Color, the most important and least costly of all the elements of design, is considered in some detail in part three.

Light

Light, both natural and artificial, is an essential element in every interior and should be given special attention in the initial planning of the room. The effect of natural light on color is discussed in part three. For artificial light, sufficient and conveniently placed outlets should be an integral part of the architectural planning, and all fixtures and lamps should be integrated with the furnishings of the room. Our visual comfort and general mood are influenced by the amount, source, and quality of illumination. With the great variety of today's artificial lighting, both incandescent and florescent, lighting has become a more important aspect of space. At one's disposal are delicately tinted globes; lighting systems that throw light upward, downward, or in both directions; dimmers that give soft overall lighting; and spotlights that dramatize specific areas. Effects to be achieved through a knowledgeable use of lighting are endless.

A number of excellent lighting brochures on the market today can help you with your lighting problems. The National Education Association of the United States in Washington, D. C., publishes a handbook on light and sight. The American Home Lighting Institute in Chicago also puts out a booklet with informative and current material on home lighting.

(Above). A pleasing use of rectangular and curved lines is used in this conversation area. Intimacy is encouraged, and clutter has been avoided. *Courtesy of Lane.*

(Below). Accessories are the most revealing of all home furnishings. Choose each lamp with the greatest care. These lamps are well-designed and extremely versatile. *Courtesy of Ethan Allen.*

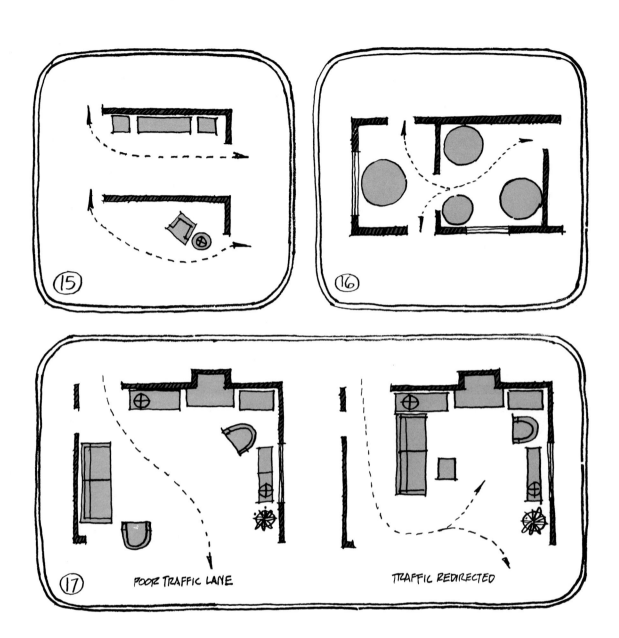

POOR TRAFFIC LANE   TRAFFIC REDIRECTED

Electric companies, too, have valuable publications available for the asking. Become informed about light and lighting fixtures.

Arranging Furniture

If each room were well designed, that is, if the proportions were pleasing, if openings were well placed, if there were no unsightly jogs, and if other architectural features were kept to a minimum and were well designed, placing the furniture in a room would be a simple matter. Unfortunately, too often the room is not well designed and must be furnished in such a way as to minimize defects and take advantage of the good points.

Rooms are for people to live in, to move about in, and to carry on activities in. Therefore, the well-being of individuals and the purposes for which the room is planned should be the major concerns of a room's arrangement. Design principles should furnish guidelines, but common sense should be the paramount influence. Rooms can be beautiful, yet impossible to live in. When you are arranging furniture, practicality and efficiency should have first priority.

Guidelines

- Plan each room with its purpose in mind. Decide what the room will be used for and by whom.
- Use furniture in keeping with the scale of the room itself. The overall dimensions and the architectural background should determine the size and general feeling of the furnishings.
- Provide space for traffic. Doorways should be free (15). Major traffic lanes must be unobstructed by furniture (16). It is sometimes necessary to redirect traffic (17), and this can be accomplished by skillful furniture placement and by the use of screens and dividers.
- Arrange furnishings to give the room a sense of equilibrium. Opposite walls should *seem* the same so that the room will be at rest. Where neither architectural features nor furniture distribution can create this feeling, it may be achieved through the knowledgeable use of color, fabrics, and accessories. In a room where the ceiling is slanted, the heaviest furniture grouping should be against the highest wall.
- Achieve a good balance of high and low and angular and rounded furniture. Where furniture is all or predominantly low, the feeling of height may be created by incorporating shelves, mirrors, pictures, and hangings in a grouping.
- Consider architectural and mechanical features. There should be no interference with opening windows, swinging doors, or heating or air-conditioning devices. Lamps should be placed near electrical outlets and out of the lines of traffic.
- Do not overcrowd a room. It is always better to be underfurnished than overfurnished. Some empty space between groupings helps to give an uncluttered effect. An occasional open space or empty corner may enhance a room and give the occupants breathing space. On the other hand, a room may

33

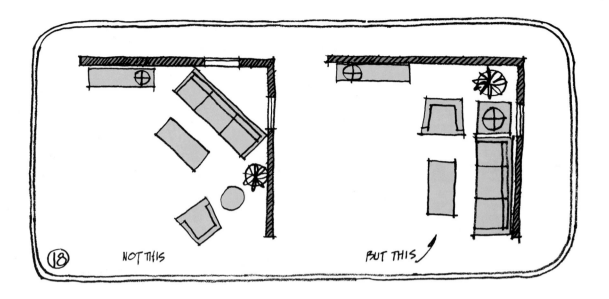

NOT THIS   BUT THIS

be too stark and uninviting. Avoid either extreme.

■ Large pieces of furniture must always be placed parallel to the walls. Crossing a corner with a sofa or case piece gives a room a disturbing feeling; an exception is large upholstered chairs, which often look better at an angle (18).

■ General reminders: Use line skillfully. Avoid pushing large pieces of furniture tightly into a corner (19) or too close to floor-to-ceiling windows where a passageway should be allowed. Arrange furniture in groups according to function, with all necessary items conveniently placed. Provide adequate lighting for all activities that will take place in the room.

Some Special Considerations

■ The conversation area. The most important group in the living room should be the conversation area. This is usually combined with and enhances the focal point, while in some cases the conversation area itself is the focal point of the room. In most living rooms and family rooms, the conversation area is focused around the fireplace. The main thing to keep in mind when planning the conversation area is that its function is to provide an intimate grouping, out of the line of traffic, in which people can hear and be heard in a relaxed atmosphere. The optimum distance across this area should be about eight feet, but plans should be made for converting this into a larger grouping by including occasional chairs that have been located at convenient points.

Built-in seating is not usually as comfortable nor as flexible as sofas and chairs that may be regrouped for more intimate occasions or opened out to invite more participants. An angled or slightly curved sofa lends itself to easy conversation more than a long, straight one.

Chairs should be comfortable and not all the same type or size. Since

COLORPLATE 5. Fun and glamour in a one-room apartment. Jungle prints on beds, pillows, and at window; non-skid fake fur rug, wicker, knotty pine, and matchstick shades create a corner with a beat. *Courtesy of Imperial Wallcoverings and Collins and Aikman.*

COLORPLATE 6. A storage wall with carefully planned space and a well-lighted spot for reading and working contribute to the efficiency and pleasure of living. *Courtesy of Armstrong Cork Company.*

COLORPLATE 7. (Above). Good taste is planning your color schemes. Here soft green and white are used to establish a transition from bedroom to dressing room, but without monotony. *Courtesy of Imperial Wallcoverings and Collins and Aikman.* **(Below).** For the timeless country look of Early American these pieces are functional and well-designed. *Courtesy of Ethan Allen.*

37

(19) NOT THIS   BUT THIS ✦

people are built differently, what is comfortable for one person may be uncomfortable for another. Place chairs to look inviting. If they are too rigidly placed, they may give a guest the uneasy feeling that to alter the placement may be a major calamity. Near each lounge chair and sofa an appropriate table should be conveniently placed to hold a lamp and small items, such as books, magazines, and light refreshments.

■ Placing the piano. Finding the right wall space for a piano is often a problem, but an upright piano need not stand against a wall as has been its usual place. Try placing it at right angles to a wall with a low screen behind it. The screen will serve as a background for a small chair and table. If the piano is low, back it up to a sofa, thus providing a convenient surface for a lamp, and the player can then face the room. An upright piano may also serve as a room divider. Dress up the back with a piece of fabric that blends with the room (20).

COLORPLATE 8. Good taste is decorating appropriately. What could be more appropriate than this room for two young girls? *Courtesy of Imperial Wallcoverings and Collins and Aikman.*

39

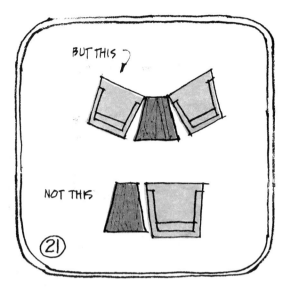

■ The function of small tables. In the living room most tables should be used only where there is a functional need. The scale, shape, and height of each table must be right not only for the chair or sofa it accompanies but also for its purpose. A triangular shaped table belongs between two chairs that are turned to create an intimate conversation group — not beside a single chair or sofa (21). Console or side tables can be decorative as well as functional and, when combined with a mirror or picture, are an asset to almost any room. The game table is usually a folding type, but where a permanent one is used, it may serve other purposes, such as for study or for company snacks. The writing-table desk gives a room a lived-in appearance and may also serve a dual purpose. Placed with its short side to the wall near a window or as part of a wall of books, it is more convenient and usually contributes more to the general attractiveness of the room than when pushed flat against a wall.

■ Large case pieces such as chests, cupboards, bookcases, and stereos should be conveniently located and placed to give the room a feeling of balance. If the wall area is small, large pieces of furniture are better if centered. Where wall space is ample, a large piece may be balanced by a grouping of smaller items.

When the Room is Small

A common problem with many families today is the need for more space. There never seems to be enough. People get bigger, homes seem to get smaller, and the costs go up. What to do?

Through the adroit use of the principles of design, it is possible to transform a room to appear much larger than it actually is. Space-expanding colors (see part three),

40

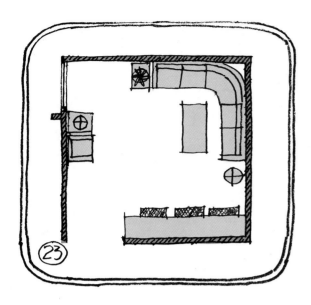

three-dimensional wallpapers, plain wall-to-wall floor coverings, and carefully selected and arranged furniture will work wonders.

■ When selecting furniture, choose the following:

    Small-scale items

    High, shallow pieces for storage and display

    Tables with rounded corners, glass, or plastic tops

    Chairs without arms and with see-through backs

    Upholstered pieces without skirts (22)

    Case pieces on legs rather than flush to the floor.

■ When arranging furniture, align furniture against the wall, leaving the center of the room free (23). Hang shelves and high storage units from the ceiling and stop approximately a foot from the floor, thus allowing the perimeter to be seen. Smaller units such as serving tables, consoles, buffets, and desks may be hung to the wall, thus eliminating the need for legs.

■ The use of dual purpose furniture will utilize space to the best advantage. For example, a coffee table with a quick change from short to long screw-on legs becomes a dining table, a desk becomes a server for a buffet supper, a sofa may have underneath storage and serves as a bed, a chair may have a back that flips over to form a table. Use your imagination in building simple items of furniture to serve a variety of needs.

The problems of space are often compounded after a year or two of married life. Take a one-room apartment planned and arranged for two people, a man and a woman. Then add one baby. Where to find space? Don't panic! Clear out a closet, push back or remove the doors, and a crib will fit in snugly. Under the crib there will be room enough for a fabric-covered box to hold baby clothes. Space over the water closet in the bathroom can be utilized for shelves for all the necessary toilet articles. Look around you. With

Room	Clearance
Living Room	
Traffic — major	
Traffic path — minor	4' to 6'
Foot room between sofa or chair and edge of coffee table top	1'4" to 4' 1' to 15"
Floor space in front of chair for feet and legs	1'6" to 2'6"
Chair or bench space in front of desk or piano	3'
Dining Room	
Space for occupied chairs	1'6" to 1'10"
Space to get into chairs	1'10" to 3'
For gentlemen to help	4'6"
Traffic path around table and occupied chairs	1'6" to 2'
Kitchen	
Working space in front of cabinets	2'6" to 6'
Counter space between equipment	3' to 5'
Ventilation or attachments at back for some	3" to 5"
Bedroom	
Space for making bed	1'6" to 2'
Space between twin beds	3' to 5'
Space in front of chest of drawers	3'
Space in front of dresser	3' to 4' (both directions)
Bathroom	
Space between front of tub and opposite walls	2'6" to 3'6"
Space in front of toilet	1'6" to 2'
Space at sides of toilet	1' to 1'6"
Space between fixtures	2' to 3'

careful organization, often room can be found where there seems to be none. Efficient use of space takes planning, but the result is worth the extra effort.

Furniture Clearances

When arranging or installing furniture, keep in mind that people require space. Listed below are some of the *minimum* dimensions necessary for clearance.

Personalize Your Walls

Bare walls staring at you in a sparsely furnished living room cry out for some kind of enrichment. But what? The art you choose to live with and display is probably the most personal thing in your home and tells more about you than any single thing. The woman decorating her home on a restricted budget may have a particular need to beautify her walls to make up for a lack of furnishings. Here is where imagination and creativity are needed. The items that can be grouped together to create an artistic wall composition are unlimited, and there are no specific rules about what to or what not to put together, or how it should be done. But that intangible quality of good taste must be employed if the result is to be a comfortable one. Keep in mind that a wall composition is under constant view and must not be overpowering.

As you stand back in the room and view the wall, each element you see against it, such as chairs, benches, tables, lamps, and hanging lights, must be included in the composition. As you plan your arrangement, keep in mind that the room's architectural features must be considered; scale, proportion, and balance are of special importance; straight lines should be relieved by curved lines; rectangles and ovals are more pleasing than squares and circles; and that uneven numbers are more desirable than even numbers.

Wall texture and pattern must determine, to some degree, the items to be placed against it. Rough texture requires heavier objects than smooth texture. Large-scale, patterned wallpapers call for wall-hung items equally as large. If a picture is small, separate it from the patterned background with a mat to give it importance.

If a single picture is hung, it deserves special consideration. Remember the golden mean. Avoid having the center of the picture midway between floor and ceiling. A single picture must not seem to float by itself but must be part of a grouping, well related in scale to the piece of furniture which forms the anchor, and hung at a pleasing height. For example, a picture hung above a lounge chair should be neither too small nor too large, should be placed high enough that the head of a seated person does not touch the frame — approximately six to eight inches will provide sufficient clearance — but not so high that it ceases to be a part of the group (24). If a picture is important enough to be hung, it should be seen and not obscured by an accessory, such as a lamp or a bouquet of flowers. Good pictures need not be expensive. There are excellent traditional prints on

43

PICTURE FLOATS HERE   PICTURE TOO SMALL   PICTURE TOO LARGE   PICTURE WELL SCALED

24

the market for very little money, and a good print is better than a mediocre original. If you love contemporary art, there is an enormous range from which to choose.

A favorite practice today is to group art and other small accessories on the largest unoccupied wall space above a large piece of furniture. In the living room the sofa is the most logical place. To assemble the components, use a large sheet of brown wrapping paper the size of the wall area to be covered. Lay the paper on the floor and arrange the pictures and other objects on it until the composition is pleasing to you. Draw around each object and mark the point where it is to be hung. Next, carefully attach the paper to the wall and proceed to hang the pictures. When all are in place, remove the paper, and your composition is complete.

If you would like an attractive wall display and your budget is limited, do not despair. There are likely a number of items among your possessions that could be assembled with charming effect. Put your imagination to work and do some experimenting. You will have fun doing it.

Do your own framing. A picture can be enhanced or destroyed by the way it is framed. To achieve the most pleasing result is more complex than one might suspect, but with a little study and observation it can be accomplished. Some pictures do not call for a frame but are complete without. Where a frame is used, it should never dominate the picture but should be carefully chosen to be appropriate for the subject and the style of rendering. Frames can repeat wood tones of furniture, or they can be painted or gilded. A traditional oil demands a rich, heavy frame, and all oils should be framed without mats. Pencil sketches, etchings, and watercolors are more

delicate and should be simply framed and usually matted. Watch for used frames at thrift stores and garage sales, and search the family attic; you may find a treasure.

A mat will make a picture look larger; it will "tie together" pictures of various sizes, and it may be a transition between picture and wall. White mats are usually preferred because they emphasize the picture, but mats may be chosen to pick up colors in the picture or in the room. When matting a picture, consider the size of the picture and the wall space where it is to be hung. When matting a square picture, leave the same space at the top and the sides with a wider margin at the bottom. For an upright rectangle, leave a medium margin at the top, the narrowest at the sides, and widest at the bottom. A rectangle frame, hung horizontally, should have a narrow margin at the top, medium at the sides, and wide at the bottom (25). Once the picture is correctly framed, it should be carefully

hung to be seen and enjoyed. Hang it flat against the wall with the cord concealed. Dipping the nail in ice water before pounding it in the wall will prevent cracking the plaster.

The items that can be hung on walls to give character to a room are without number and are determined only by personal taste. Make a handsome collage: press and mount flowers and leaves, frame them identically, and hang them in a group. Make a lighted shadow box from an old picture frame lined with fabric, and display in it small memorabilia. Group small pictures on a piece of plywood covered with velvet. Whatever you hang on your wall, let it frankly reflect your taste, and place it so that it looks as if it were meant for that very spot, remembering that suitability and simplicity are the keys to success.

These, then, are the elements of "good taste." You will be surprised at how quickly you can develop your own pleasing designs.

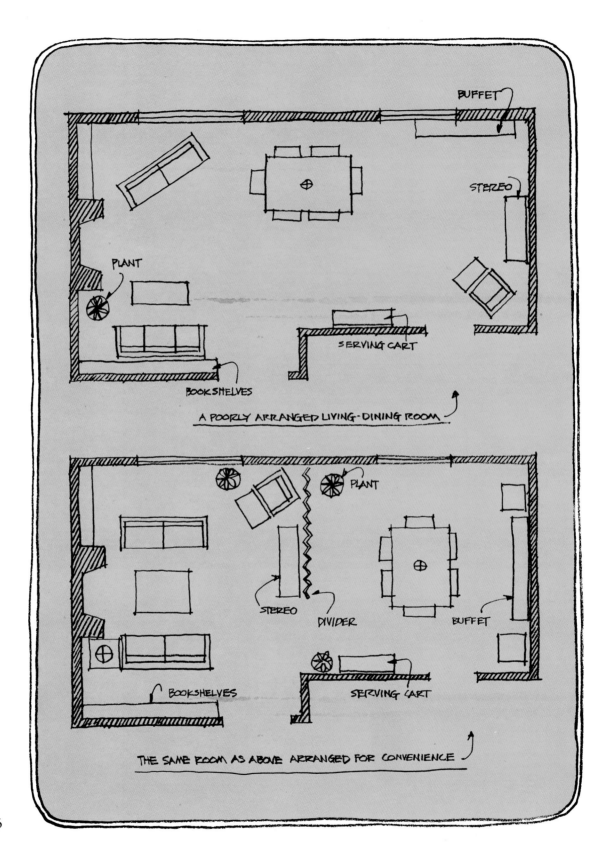

BUFFET

STEREO

PLANT

SERVING CART

BOOKSHELVES

A POORLY ARRANGED LIVING-DINING ROOM

PLANT

STEREO

DIVIDER

BUFFET

BOOKSHELVES

SERVING CART

THE SAME ROOM AS ABOVE ARRANGED FOR CONVENIENCE

Suggestions and Assignments for Part Two: Developing Good Taste

Suggested Teaching Aids and Procedures

1. Illustrate principles of design with good and bad examples.
2. Use three-dimensional furniture kit to illustrate furniture arrangement.
3. Show illustrations of good and bad wall compositions.

Student Assignments

1. Using the squared paper and templates referred to in the accompanying instructions, plan the two rooms with efficient use of space. Keep in mind the guidelines for furniture arranging.

2. Take a critical look at the furniture in your living room and bedroom at home. Make a scale drawing of each room. Using the templates, arrange the furniture to best fill the functional needs of each room, with an eye to good design.

3. Using the wall and furniture silhouettes, make two wall compositions: one that illustrates bisymmetrical balance and one that illustrates asymmetrical balance. You may wish to use a wall in your own room.

4. Look carefully at the walls in your living room at home. Can you make some constructive criticism?

5. Complete work sheets 1, 2, 3.

Working Materials

1. Squared paper 1 square 1/4″ = 1′
2. Furniture templates 1/4″ = 1′
3. Furniture silhouettes

Work Sheets 1, 2, 3

Objective

The objective of these projects is to give the student: first, an opportunity to demonstrate his or her skill in arranging furniture in an artistic, and at the same time functional, manner; second, an opportunity to use his or her artistic skill in creating pleasing wall compositions in which both bisymmetrical balance and asymmetrical balance are used.

Instruction to Students

Work sheets 1 and 2. Using the accompanying templates, place the furniture in each of the two rooms to create pleasing and functional arrangements. Follow the guidelines that are given in the lesson material for furniture arranging.

Work sheet 3. Using the attached silhouettes, make a pleasing wall composition on each of the two walls on work sheet 3. Use architectural elements, furniture, and wall-hung items. Wall (a): here, make a bisymmetrical arrangement. Wall (b): here, make an asymmetrical arrangement.

47

Floor Plan Graph
Each square equals one square foot:
Scale ¼" = 1'.

Floor Plan Graph
Each square equals one square foot:
Scale ¼" = 1'.

LIVING ROOM

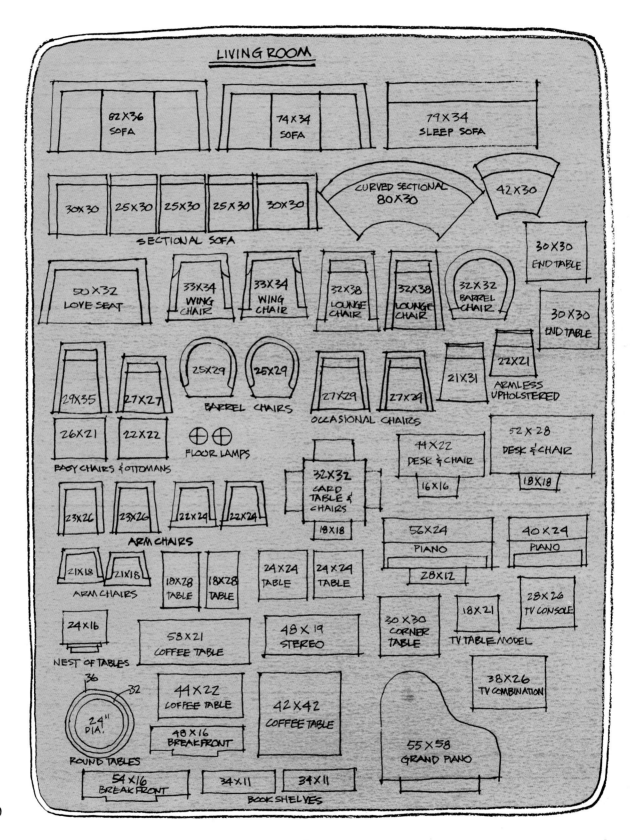

82 X 36 SOFA

74 X 34 SOFA

79 X 34 SLEEP SOFA

30X30 25X30 25X30 25X30 30X30
SECTIONAL SOFA

CURVED SECTIONAL 80X30

42X30

30 X 30 END TABLE

50 X 32 LOVE SEAT

33X34 WING CHAIR

33X34 WING CHAIR

32X38 LOUNGE CHAIR

32X38 LOUNGE CHAIR

32X32 BARREL CHAIR

30 X 30 END TABLE

29X35

27X27

25X29 25X29
BARREL CHAIRS

27X29 27X29
OCCASIONAL CHAIRS

21X31

22X21 ARMLESS UPHOLSTERED

26X21

22X22

FLOOR LAMPS

EASY CHAIRS & OTTOMANS

32X32 CARD TABLE & CHAIRS

18X18

44X22 DESK & CHAIR

16X16

52 X 28 DESK & CHAIR

18X18

23X26 23X26 22X24 22X24
ARM CHAIRS

56X24 PIANO

28X12

40 X 24 PIANO

21X18 21X18
ARM CHAIRS

18X28 TABLE

18X28 TABLE

24 X 24 TABLE

24 X 24 TABLE

18X21

28X26 TV CONSOLE

24 X 16

NEST OF TABLES

58 X 21 COFFEE TABLE

48 X 19 STEREO

30 X 30 CORNER TABLE

TV TABLE MODEL

36
32
24" DIA.
ROUND TABLES

44 X 22 COFFEE TABLE

48 X 16 BREAKFRONT

42 X 42 COFFEE TABLE

38X26 TV COMBINATION

55 X 58 GRAND PIANO

54 X 16 BREAKFRONT

34X11

34X11

BOOK SHELVES

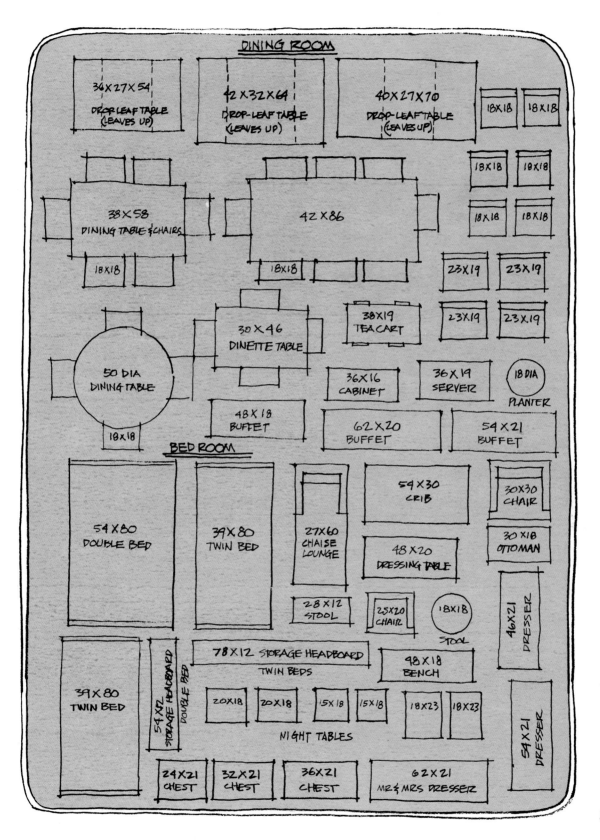

DINING ROOM

36X27X54
DROP-LEAF TABLE
(LEAVES UP)

42X32X64
DROP-LEAF TABLE
(LEAVES UP)

40X27X70
DROP-LEAF TABLE
(LEAVES UP)

18X18   18X18

18X18   18X18

18X18   18X18

38X58
DINING TABLE & CHAIRS

42X86

18X18

18X18

23X19   23X19

23X19   23X19

30X46
DINETTE TABLE

38X19
TEA CART

50 DIA
DINING TABLE

36X16
CABINET

36X19
SERVER

18 DIA
PLANTER

18X18

48X18
BUFFET

62X20
BUFFET

54X21
BUFFET

BED ROOM

54X80
DOUBLE BED

39X80
TWIN BED

27X60
CHAISE
LOUNGE

59X30
CRIB

30X30
CHAIR

48X20
DRESSING TABLE

30X18
OTTOMAN

28X12
STOOL

25X20
CHAIR

18X18
STOOL

46X21
DRESSER

39X80
TWIN BED

54X21
STORAGE HEADBOARD
DOUBLE BED

78X12 STORAGE HEADBOARD
TWIN BEDS

98X18
BENCH

20X18   20X18   15X18   15X18   18X23   18X23

NIGHT TABLES

54X21
DRESSER

24X21
CHEST

32X21
CHEST

36X21
CHEST

62X21
MR & MRS DRESSER

51

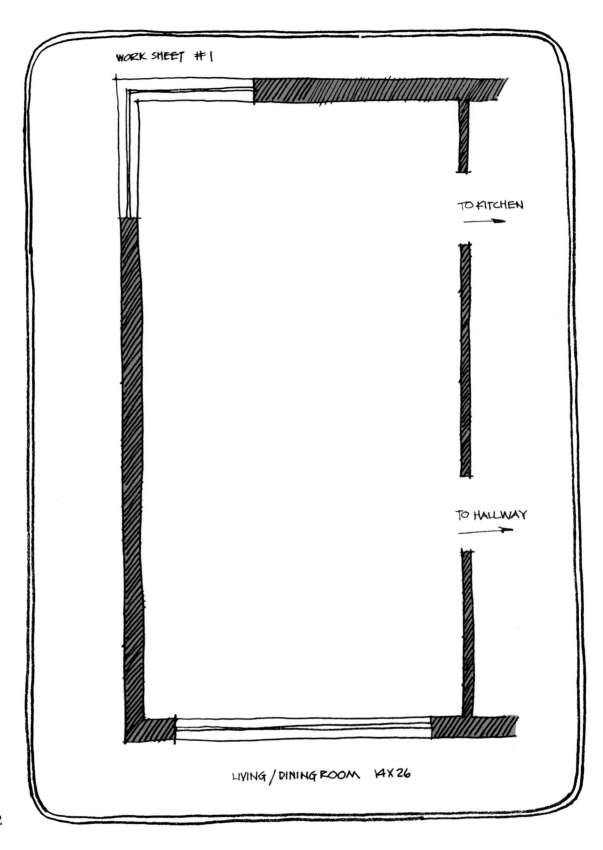

WORK SHEET #1

TO KITCHEN

TO HALLWAY

LIVING / DINING ROOM 14 X 26

52

NAME _____

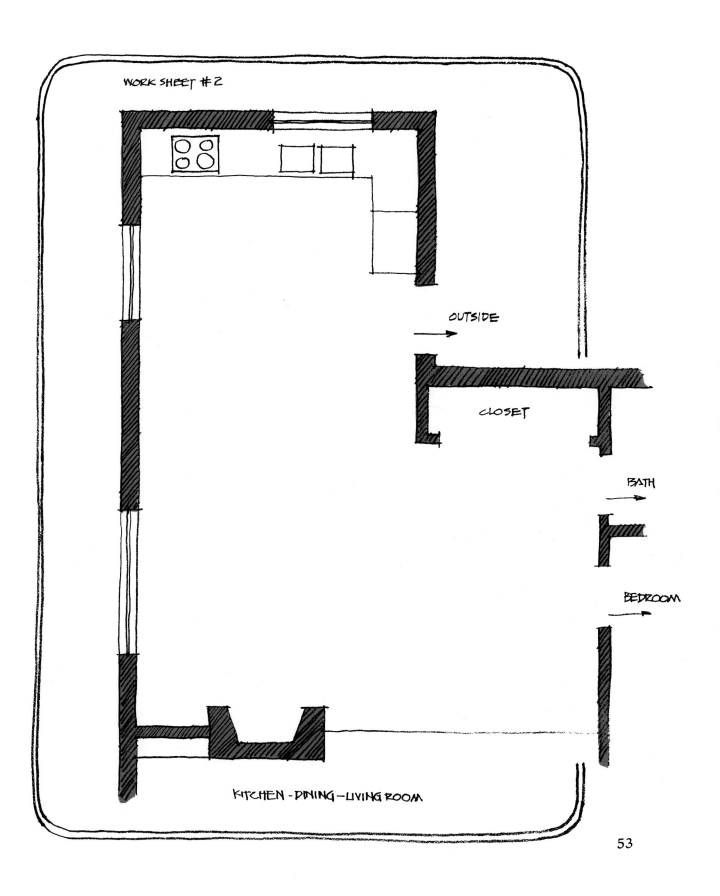

WORK SHEET #2

OUTSIDE

CLOSET

BATH

BEDROOM

KITCHEN - DINING - LIVING ROOM

53

NAME _____

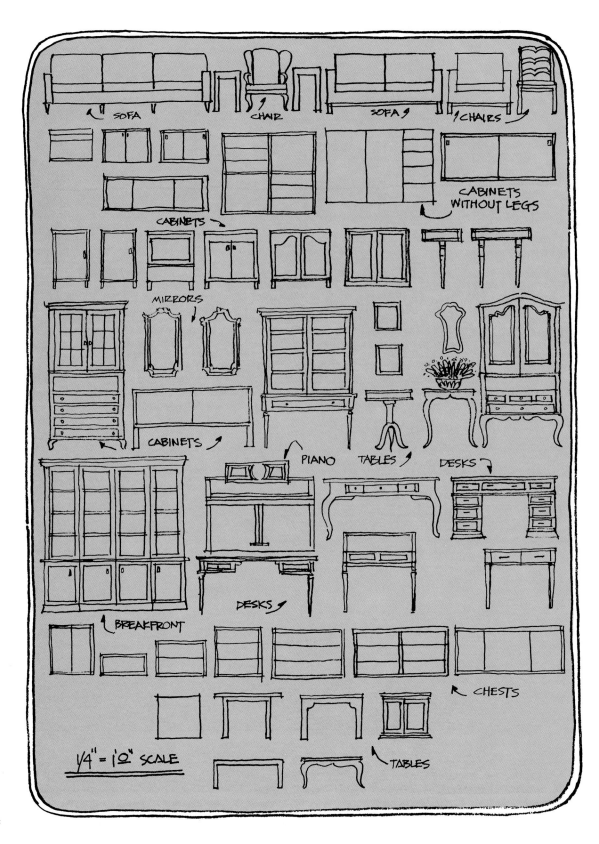

SOFA   CHAIR   SOFA   CHAIRS

CABINETS WITHOUT LEGS

CABINETS

MIRRORS

CABINETS   PIANO   TABLES   DESKS

DESKS

BREAKFRONT

CHESTS

1/4" = 1'0" SCALE   TABLES

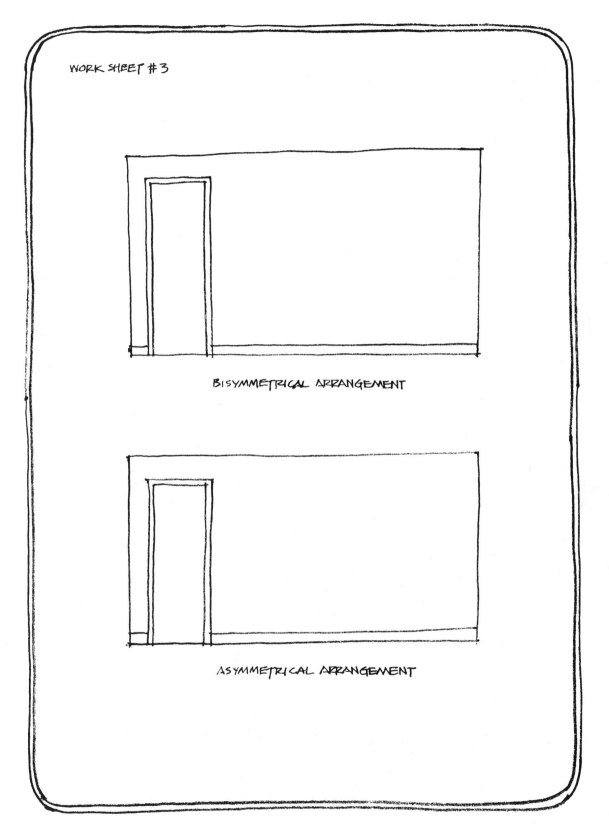

BISYMMETRICAL ARRANGEMENT

ASYMMETRICAL ARRANGEMENT

NAME _____

Your Own Color Schemes

COLORPLATE 9. This entrancing room with its one-color scheme will delight both young and old. Coordinated fabric and wall covering unify the room. Vinyl brick floor adds a sturdy look, and lacy wicker and daisies complete the setting. *Courtesy of Imperial Wallcoverings and Collins and Aikman.*

Being your own color schemer does not mean that you should disregard all the principles you have learned about color. True, there are no absolutes, and there is no such thing as a bad color if it is properly used. But to interpret "be your own color schemer" or "do your own color thing" as meaning that anything and everything goes, is to invite disappointment.

Your own personal color scheme, to be satisfying to you, must be based on some understanding of how colors work together. Developing a satisfactory color scheme is never easy. The result should be comfortable and livable, and it may even look as though it were put together without any effort. However, anyone who has worked with color knows that this is not so. Examine the colors in any successful room, and you will find that they follow a disciplined plan. Learn the basic principles of color scheming and then develop your own plan.

Color Is Your Most Important Tool; Make It Work for You

Color is the least costly and the most important element in your decorative scheme, but its success depends upon a working knowledge of certain basic rules and their relationship to people. Each color contains properties peculiar to itself; these properties produce certain psychological effects.

The reason people are affected by certain colors is not clearly understood, but we do know that peoples' emotions are greatly influenced by color and that women are more sensitive to color than men.

Know the Color Wheel

The challenge of color should be faced head-on, with a determination to learn how to make it work for you. To begin with, learn the color wheel.

If you draw a line through the standard color wheel, the colors on one side tend to be warm; those on the other

59

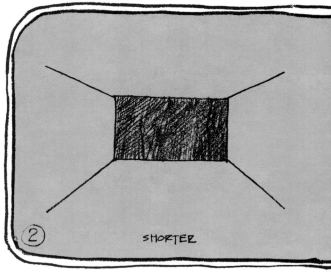

side tend to be cool (1). Warm colors
are active and cheery, and tend to advance, thus filling up space. Cool
colors are generally restful and soothing and seem to push out and open up
space. Because of this, warm colors
tend to make rooms feel smaller; cool
colors tend to make rooms appear larger.
Keep these properties in mind when
you are choosing colors for any room.

Colors which fall midway between warm and cool are called neutrals. Neutral colors are important to
every color scheme. Warm neutrals are
easier to work with than cool neutrals.
Large background areas of warm
neutral tones tend to produce the most
livable and lasting color schemes.

By using this principle of color, not
only can a decorator change the
apparent overall size of a room, but he
can visually alter the proportion. For
example, a long, narrow room can be
made to appear shorter if the end walls
are painted or paneled in warmer,
darker tones than the side walls (2).
A square room can appear as a
rectangle if two of the opposite sides
are lighter than the remaining two.

A close look at the color wheel will
show that it is based on three primary
colors — yellow, red, and blue —
called primary because they cannot be
mixed from other pigments, nor can
they be broken down into component
colors. By adding equal amounts of
any two of the primary colors, the result is three secondary colors. In
similar fashion, six tertiary hues are
made by mixing equal amounts of a
primary color and a secondary color.
These 12 hues comprise the full color
wheel. To know how to use it is to
know the ABC's of color.

There is no magic about the use of
color and no short cut to acquiring that

60

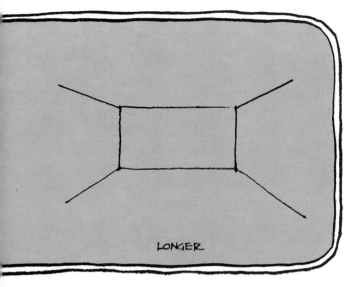

LONGER

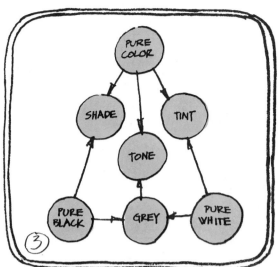

③

"sense of color" some people seem to have. But it is nevertheless true that you can become skilled at using color. When you have learned a few simple color facts and principles, you will have at your disposal a valuable tool with which to create your own kind of beauty.

Color's Three Dimensions

When you understand the color wheel and how to use it, learn color terminology. Learn about color's three dimensions and about shades and tints. Learn about hue, value, and intensity. *Hue* is the color name. *Value* is the darkness or lightness of a color in relation to black and white. *Intensity* describes the brightness or dullness of a color or the amount of pure color it contains. *Shades* are hues to which black has been added. *Tints* are hues to which white has been added. *Tones* are formed by adding both black and

white or some of the color's direct complement (3).

In every room there should be a variety of values — dark, light, and medium. A different mood can be established when value is distributed differently (4).

No guide to the use of color is more important than neutralization. Too much intense color is difficult to live with and can be psychologically irritating. More dull than bright is a good rule to follow.

To reduce the amount of intensity in a color, neutralize: add some of that color's complement. There are many degrees of neutralization, the number varying with different hues. When equal amounts of two complementary colors are mixed, they neutralize each other. A safe rule to follow when color-scheming a room is to use the most neutralized hues on the largest areas — walls and floor. As the area decreases in size — with sofas, large chairs,

61

windows — the intensity may increase, with the most intense hues reserved for the accessories, such as pillows. This is known as the law of chromatic distribution and is the safest rule to follow in creating livable rooms.

Color Scheming

There are no absolutes about combining colors, but a knowledge of basic reliable color schemes can be helpful. In general, all color schemes fall into two categories: related or contrasting. Within these, the variations are endless. Related colors produce harmonious schemes which may be cool, warm, or a combination of both. Contrasting schemes have great variety and tend to be more exciting, particularly if strong intensity is used. In any scheme, black or white or both may be added without changing the scheme.

The three basic color schemes are technically known as monochromatic, analogous, and complementary. *Monochromatic* is a single color scheme (5). Various tints, shades, and intensities must be used to avoid monotony. The most notable thing about this type of scheme is unity. There is, however, a danger that a one-color scheme may become monotonous. Monotony may be avoided, however, by the use of striking textures in fabrics and by the use of metals, woods, and glass. The *analogous* color scheme is produced from any segment of colors which are side by side on the color wheel (6). There must be not fewer than three and not more than six colors. Analogous color schemes may be either cool or warm. They are easy, natural, and comfortable to live with and have a natural harmony dependent always on the amount of intensity and the distribution of value. The *complementary* color scheme is composed of colors that lie opposite on the color wheel. It is a contrasty scheme and contains both cool and warm colors. It may be lively or subdued, depending upon the intensity of the colors.

There are five complementary color schemes: direct, split, triad, double, and alternate. *Direct complement* is the simplest of the contrastive color schemes and is formed by using any two colors which lie directly opposite on the color wheel (7). *Split complement* is a three-color scheme composed of any hue plus the two hues which are next to its complement (8). *Triad color scheme* is another three-color contrasting scheme. The triad is made up of any three colors that are equidistant from one another on the color wheel (9). *Double complement* is a four-color scheme in which two pairs of complementary colors are used (10). *Alternate complement* is another four-color scheme which combines the triad and the direct complement (11).

In addition to the three basic color schemes above, many other ways exist of developing livable schemes. One of the most successful methods is to start with a fabric. Pick a multicolored cotton or a subtle damask, whichever strikes your fancy. Then choose one of the lightest colors, neutralize it, and use it for the walls. The floor may be

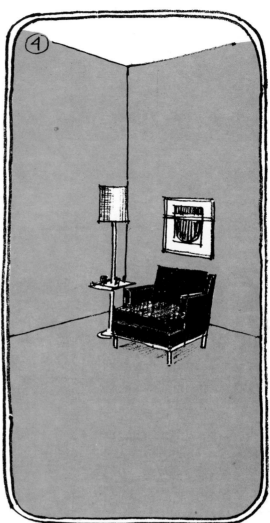

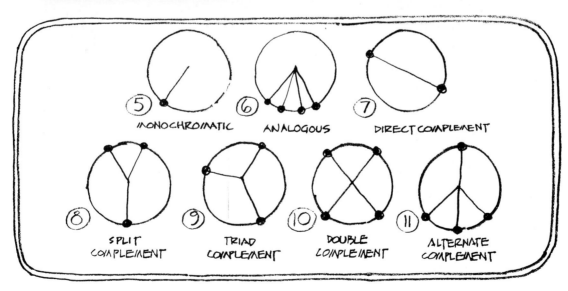

⑤ MONOCHROMATIC

⑥ ANALOGOUS

⑦ DIRECT COMPLEMENT

⑧ SPLIT COMPLEMENT

⑨ TRIAD COMPLEMENT

⑩ DOUBLE COMPLEMENT

⑪ ALTERNATE COMPLEMENT

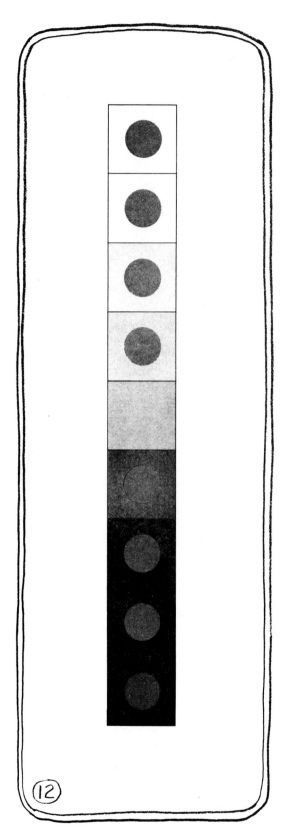

closely blended to the walls or a deeper shade of the walls or one of the contrasting colors in the fabric. Use one or more of the stronger colors for the larger pieces of furniture and reserve the most intense colors for the room's accents, such as pillows.

Wallpaper, a rug, or a painting may be the source of the color scheme; if so, follow the same procedure as with a fabric. Whatever method of color scheming you use, keep in mind the little rhyme: "something dark and something light, something dull and something bright" — referring to value and intensity.

Other Things You Should Know about Color

▪ One cannot judge a color by itself. The most important thing to remember about color is that *colors affect each other*; changes occur when colors are brought together. Observe in the accompanying illustration what occurs when the background behind a grey circle is changed from black to white (12). Before deciding on any colored item, take it home and see what happens when it is in your own environment. For example, the little slipper chair that was a soft green in the store looks too bright in your own bedroom. What caused the change? In the store the green chair was placed against a more intense green background; your bedroom wall is pink. The answer: *a neutral color will appear even more neutral if placed against a background of the same color with more saturation.* This is what you saw in the store. On the other hand, *a color will appear more intense when placed against its com-*

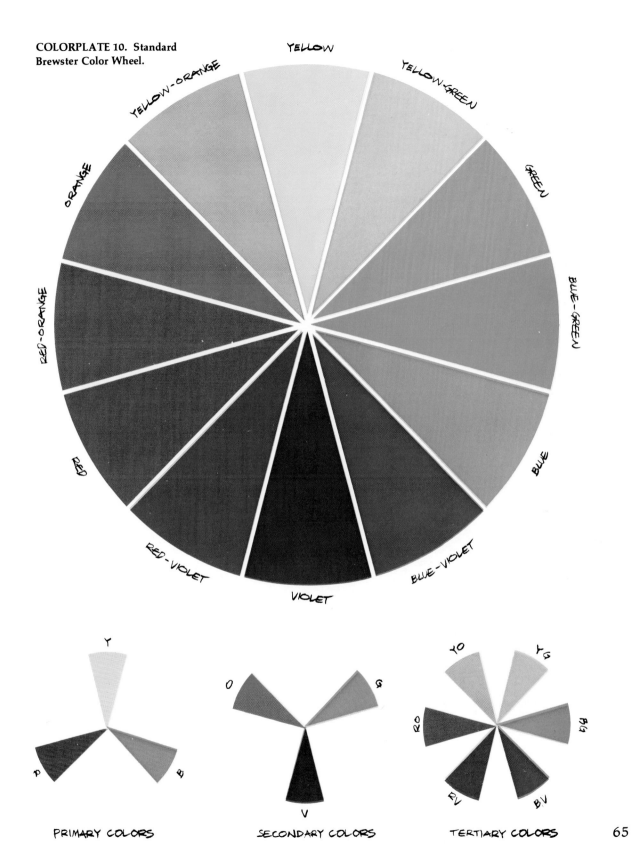

COLORPLATE 10. Standard Brewster Color Wheel.

YELLOW

YELLOW-ORANGE

YELLOW-GREEN

ORANGE

GREEN

RED-ORANGE

BLUE-GREEN

RED

BLUE

RED-VIOLET

BLUE-VIOLET

VIOLET

PRIMARY COLORS

SECONDARY COLORS

TERTIARY COLORS

65

COLORPLATE 11. Dark walls
absorb color, but the sharp blues
and reds can hold their own here.
Color transition is attractively
planned. *Courtesy of Armstrong
Cork Company.*

plement or a contrasty color. This is what you had in your own room. Following are other examples showing what happens when colors are brought together. If a picture with neutralized blue colors is placed against a blue wall of the same hue but with more intensity, the picture will appear even more neutral. If the same picture is placed against a wall painted in its complementary or a contrasty color (gold), it will appear to be a more intense blue. If you select a striped fabric for your sofa in which the stripe is a complement of the background color, and they both have the same value and intensity, they will clash. If the value of one of the colors is changed, it will *not* clash even though the intensity remains the same.

These examples show that both intensity and value are affected by their neighbors. So always try fabrics in your room before making a purchase.

■ Colors in a room are affected by both natural and artificial light. The amount or quantity of natural light depends upon the number, size, and placement of the windows. The quality of natural light depends upon the direction from which the light comes. North light tends to be cool; light from the south and west are warmer; light from the east is more neutral. With this knowledge, use cooler colors in south and west rooms than in north rooms. But if your favorite color for a bedroom is blue and your room happens to be on the north, go ahead and do it in blue,

warming it up with some yellow. Because the light in every room is different, never make a purchase where color is involved without first trying it out.

Colors are also affected by artificial light. Some colors are blended by warm fluorescent light. Greens, for example, the friendliest of all colors, are more blended under warm lamp light. On the other hand, blues — the most challenging colors to work with — that look just right together during the day, may "fight" each other under artificial light. Today's artificial light has become very sophisticated and deserves careful study. When used with skill, it can alter colors in an endless number of ways.

■ Color is affected by texture. A rough texture on walls, in fabrics, or in floor coverings will appear darker than a smooth surface because of the shadows cast by the texture. Rough plaster walls may look dirty under some artificial lights.

■ Color can make objects appear larger or smaller. If something attracts the eye, it *seems* larger. So if that old hand-me-down sofa in your living room is too big for the room, make a slip cover for it using a light, neutral color, preferably blended to the background; see how it seems to shrink. If the only lounge chair in your living room is too small in scale, cover it with a lively printed cotton; it will visually increase in size and will enhance the room as well (13).

■ Color is affected by the distance and size of an area. At a distance, colors appear lighter and less intense than close up. Therefore, brighter and

67

darker colors in large rooms will seem less demanding than the same colors in small rooms. Colors appear stronger in chroma (hue and saturation) when covering large areas. For example, a small color chip may be the exact color tone you feel you want for your room; but when that tone is painted on four walls, it looks much darker because the area of that color chip has been multiplied many thousands of times.

When selecting a wall color from a small color chip, always choose one which is several tints lighter than you wish the completed room to appear. It is advisable to paint a sizable area of color on walls in opposite corners of the room and observe them in the light at different times of the day and night before making the complete application.

■ Color can bring balance into a room. If you have only one large piece of furniture that seems to weigh one end of the room down, and your budget won't allow for a major purchase, make a wall hanging of a striking fabric. Hang it on the wall opposite the furniture piece; watch the room take on a feeling of equilibrium.

■ Color can unify a room. A successful room is one in which there is one dominant color. Use your favorite color to tie together odd and unrelated objects or cover all upholstered items in the same lovely printed fabric. You may even put it at the window and on one wall. See the room become unified, with beauty and glamour as an extra bonus.

■ Color can create a mood. Whatever the mood you wish in your rooms, color can create it for you. Keep in mind that warm colors tend to be active, cheery, and informal, while cool colors tend to be restful, soothing, and somewhat formal. Let color work for you in establishing whatever mood you desire.

■ Color should reflect your personality. Each individual has color preferences, and it is important that people live with colors they enjoy. Color trends come and go, and often there is pressure to use the "in" colors with faddish combinations. Bizarre color schemes show up from time to time but are usually short lived. Whatever the color trends of the moment, the principles for using color remain the same. Let your own preference be the final judge, keeping in mind that self-expression with success is dependent upon discipline.

You have to live with your color schemes. Make them suitable for you.

Suggestions and Assignments for Part 3: Your Own Color Schemes

Suggested Teaching Aids
and Procedures

1. Have a large color wheel for demonstration.
2. Help students to become aware of colors around them and the way they are affected by them.
3. Demonstrate what happens when the background of a colored item is changed. Use sheets of colored paper.
4. Illustrate rooms that have too much intensity and rooms that are well color-schemed.
5. Impress upon students that rooms are to *live* in and should be planned with livability in mind.
6. Help students to see the importance of not being pressured into following color fads, but to choose colors that are right for them.

Student Assignments

Complete the three color projects attached. Keep in mind the neutralization of color to create livable color schemes.

Work Sheets 4, 5, 6

Objective

The objective of work sheets 4, 5, and 6 is to assist the student, through class supervision, to create livable color schemes, using his knowledge of neutralizing, blending, and contrasting colors. The result should be rooms pleasing to look at, that could be lived in and enjoyed for a long time.

Practicing here, with these work sheets, can begin to "make perfect."

Instruction to Students

Using tempera paints, complete work sheets 4, 5, and 6.

No. 4: An exercise in neutralizing colors.

1. Paint the squares in the left-hand column in the hues indicated.

2. Paint the squares in the middle column with the complementary hue of each.

3. In the third column, make three degrees of neutralization. This is done by adding a *very slight* touch of the complement to section number 1, a *slight bit* more to section number 2, and still a *slight bit* more to section number 3. CAUTION: Be sure that all sections in the far right-hand column remain neutralized shades of the original hue in the far left column and *not* muddy browns.

No. 5: An exercise in creating a *livable* color scheme, using a monochromatic or a one-color scheme. Be sure to alter the values and the intensity; the hue must remain the same.

No. 6: An exercise in creating a *livable* color scheme, using either a complementary or an analogous scheme.

Procedure for work sheets 5 and 6:

1. Carefully examine the examples of completed rooms on page 75.

2. Paint the ceilings of the room an off-white that will blend with an off-white you will use elsewhere in the room. When *white* is used in the room, paint the ceiling *white*.

3. Paint the largest areas of the room in the most *neutralized* tones, and reserve the intense colors for accents.

4. Keep in mind that each room should be done in colors with values and intensity that could be lived with for a long time.

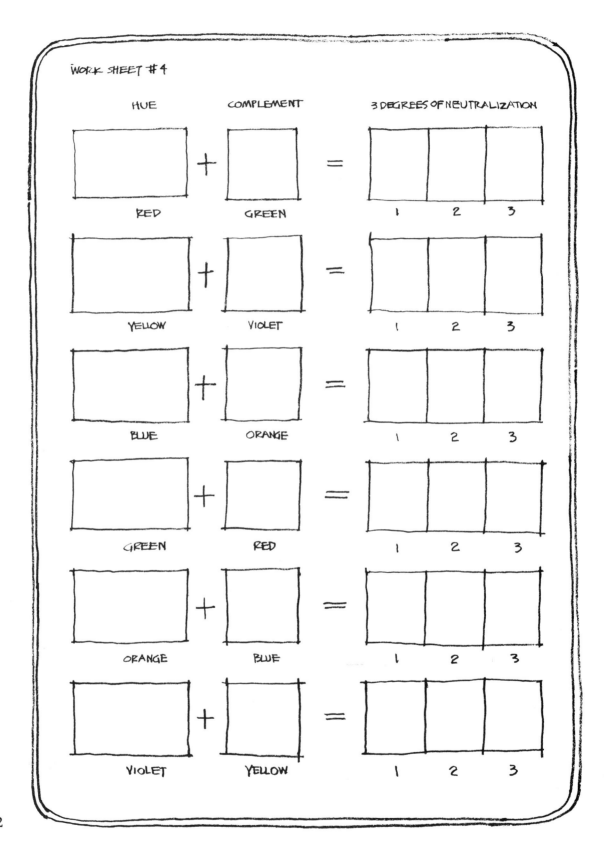

WORK SHEET #4

HUE   COMPLEMENT   3 DEGREES OF NEUTRALIZATION

RED   +   GREEN   =   1   2   3

YELLOW   +   VIOLET   =   1   2   3

BLUE   +   ORANGE   =   1   2   3

GREEN   +   RED   =   1   2   3

ORANGE   +   BLUE   =   1   2   3

VIOLET   +   YELLOW   =   1   2   3

72

NAME _____

WORK SHEET #5

73

WORK SHEET #6

74

COLORPLATE 12. The same room takes on two distinctly different moods when color is used differently. (Upper left). A traditional print used on the chair, at the window, and on two cushions sets the color scheme. The warm, neutral color is used for walls and lightened for the ceiling. The more intense color is used on the sofa, and a still more intense blue is used for accent in the pillow and lamp. The rich, brown floor holds it all together. (Upper right). A light, neutral green wall, made lighter for the ceiling and slightly more intense for the drapery, contrasts with the rich, rust floor and makes a fitting background for the deep green chair and the contemporary print on the sofa. The more intense colors are reserved for accents in the pillows, the lamp base, and the picture.

Start with Backgrounds

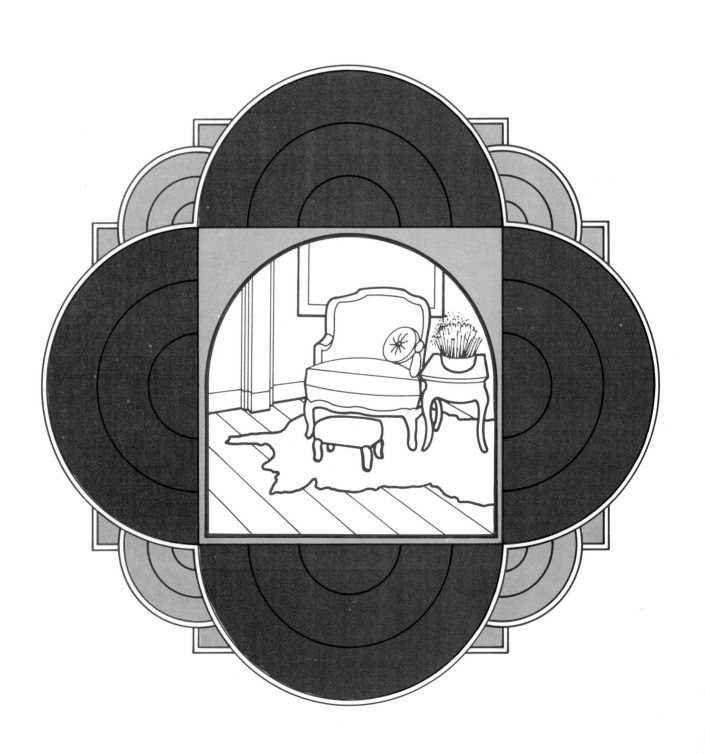

How fortunate you are to be furnishing a home today. Never before have there been so many satisfactory solutions to all the problems confronting the buyer in all categories of home furnishings. The logical place to begin furnishing a room is with the backgrounds. Since the floors and the walls are areas of the house, use and beauty determine your choice of floor coverings and wall decorations.

FLOORS

Hard Surface Flooring

The market today abounds in hard surface flooring for every room and every purpose, merging beauty and practicality. No longer is hard flooring confined to work areas; it may go anywhere in the house. Time-tested materials such as concrete, terrazzo, quarry tile, and ceramic tiles have taken on new glamour and are excellent choices for entrance halls, dining rooms,

family rooms — wherever there is hard usage. However, these floors are non-resilient and are not the best choice in areas where one spends a lot of time standing, such as the kitchen.

The development of vinyls for floor use is in large measure responsible for the new interest in hard floor coverings, since almost no limit exists to the effects which can and are being produced in vinyl: clear or vividly colored, translucent or opaque, textured or satin-smooth. Vinyls come in tiles, six-foot-wide sheets, or in a can and may be informal or formal. Small patterns mask tracking and spillage; pebble vinyls achieve a natural stone effect; and embossed patterns are reminiscent of Old World designs such as Moorish tile. Vinyls may simulate handsome grained wood, cork, delft tile, travertine, or marble, to mention only a few. One all-purpose vinyl in sheet or tile requires no adhesive. A conductive tile is made especially for hospitals and chemical and electronic laboratories as a safety against the hazard of static electricity. A foam cushion backing now makes it possible to have a practical vinyl surface with the luxurious feel of carpet.

Listed below are the most commonly used floor coverings, both nonresilient and resilient, with their characteristics and uses as well as some suggestions for the treatment and care of each to help shoppers know what to buy.

Hard Surface Flooring

Nonresilient

Material	Characteristics	Uses	Treatment and Care
Brick	Durable; requires little upkeep; comes in many textures, sizes, and colors. Brick transmits moisture and cold readily and absorbs grease unless treated.	Walks, patios, foyers, any room where a country look is desired.	Careful waxing will produce soft patina. A coating of vinyl will protect bricks from grease penetration. Dust with dry mop. Wash occasionally. For stubborn stains, use trisodium phosphate.
Flagstone	A flat stone which varies in size, thickness, quality and color. It is versatile, durable, handsome; has easy upkeep; colors range from soft grays through beiges and reddish-browns; may be cut or laid in natural shapes.	Walks, patios, foyers, any heavy traffic area. May be dressed up or down, making it appropriate for for a wide range of uses.	Treatment and care are the same as for brick.
Slate (a special kind of stone)	Tends to be more formal than flagstone. Qualities similar to flagstone except for color, which runs from gray to black.	May be used in traffic areas in rather formal rooms. Appropriate for some period rooms, particularly sun rooms and dining rooms.	May be polished or unpolished but more often waxed and highly polished.
Terrazzo	Consists of cement mortar (matrix) to which marble chips (aggregate) are mixed. Custom or precast; comes in large or small marble chips. The larger chips give a more formal appearance. Available in a limited range of colors. Sanitary, durable, and easy to clean.	Patios, foyers, halls, recreation rooms, bathrooms, or wherever traffic is heavy.	Dusting with dry mop. Occasional washing. Some varieties need occasional waxing.
Mexican Tile	Crude base with smooth surface in limited range of colors. Durable, informal, inexpensive.	Wherever a hard, cement-like surface is desired.	Care the same as for terrazzo. Surface seldom waxed.
Concrete Tile	May be solid or in squares, smooth or textured, polished or unpolished. Color may be added before pouring or after.	Particularly desirable for some hardwear areas. The tile patterns are appropriate for foyers and many areas where traffic requires extreme durability.	A heavy waxed surface is necessary for maintenance. Do not use lacquer, varnish, or shellac.

Wood floors are in a category by themselves. They are hard but resilient. Wood is the most versatile and widely used of all flooring materials. It combines beauty, warmth, resilience, resistance to indentation, durability, availability, ease of installation, and reasonable cost. The quiet harmony and beauty of oak floors provide a background for any style of furnishings; they are always in good taste. Wood has been a favorite for centuries, and

Pebble Tile	A surface in which stones are laid in concrete and polished to a smoothness, but surface remains uneven.	Especially appropriate for walks and fireplace hearths.	Dusting and occational washing.
Ceramic Tile	One of the hardest and most durable floor and wall coverings. The common type using small squares is called mosaic. It may be glazed or unglazed and comes in many colors, patterns, and textures. Glossy surface squares usually 4 1/2". New developments are producing handsome tiles 12" square with a variety of designs, textures, and colors. Ceramic tile has a unique aesthetic quality.	Especially attractive for foyers, sun rooms, bathrooms; but may be suitable for any room, depending on color, texture and period of the room.	Unglazed: may be waxed to give a soft sheen. Glazed: dust with dry mop; wash when needed with soap and warm water.
Quarry Tile	A type of ceramic tile formed and fired as it comes from the earth. One of the hardest and most durable. It may be glazed or unglazed. It is heat and frost resistant, easy to care for, and very durable. Both ceramic and quarry tile are practically impervious to grease and chemicals.	Suitable for many period rooms, especially Italian, early English, and rooms with a Mediterranean feeling. Can be used wherever a hard surface is appropriate. Its coolness makes it especially desirable in hot climates.	Care the same as for ceramic tile.
Marble	The hardest of the nonresilient flooring materials; is now available in many variaties. Marble gives a feeling of elegance. It is more expensive than most other flooring materials, but it is permanent.	Wherever elegant durability is needed. Especially appropriate with classic styles of furnishing.	Wash with soap and warm water.
Poured Seamless Vinyl	Plastic from a can, has a glossy surface, is non-slippery, and easy to maintain.	Kitchens, bathrooms, family rooms.	Does not require waxing. Clean with soap and warm water. Avoid heavy detergents.
Glass Brick	A new development, similar to glass brick for walls. It is permanent, sanitary, and translucent. Easy maintenance.	Suitable for dark areas. Adaptable to different rooms and styles.	Clean with soap and water.

Hard Surface Flooring
Resilient

Material	Characteristics	Uses	Treatment and Care
Asphalt Tile	Lowest in cost of tile group. Comes in wide range of colors. Susceptible to dents and stains. Some types are grease-resistant. Durable. Most satisfactory when laid over concrete subfloor.	Wherever hard surface, low-cost flooring is required.	A coat of water-emulsion wax will improve the surface. Use mild soap for cleaning.
Rubber Tile	Cushiony, comfortable. Exceptionally quiet. Comes in plain clear colors and marblized effects. Resists stain, but is permanently injured by gasoline, solvents, oils, grease, and strong alkalis.	Kitchen, bath, family room, utility.	Use water-emulsion wax. Avoid the use of varnish or shellac. Wash with soap and water.
Linoleum	Inlaid linoleum is durable, long-wearing, easy to clean, and quiet. Embossed linoleum has texture interest, often resembles masonry. Colors are unlimited.	Kitchen, bath, utility, entrance, family room, counter and desk tops.	Takes a high polish with wax. Avoid the use of varnish or shellac. Clean with soap and water.
Cork Tile	Cork provides maximum quiet and cushiony comfort. Cork with vinyl or urethane surface is highly resistant to wet and stains, but natural cork is not suited for the abuse of kitchen traffic or water damage. Colors are light to dark brown. Dented by furniture.	Especially appropriate for other rooms with little traffic.	Maintenance not easy. Dirt hard to dislodge from porous surface. Wash with soap and water. Coat with wax. Vinyl coating will protect the surface.
Leather Tile	Resilient, quiet, but expensive. Natural or dyed colors.	Studies and other limited areas with little traffic.	Warm water and mild soap.
Vinyl Asbestor	Excellent all-around low-cost florring. Available in tile or sheets. Resists stains and wears well. Hard and noisy. Tiles have self-adhesive backing.	May be used in any room.	Exceptionally easy to maintain.
Vinyl Cork	Has the appearance of cork, but resists stain and is easy to maintain. Colors richer than natural cork.	Wherever the effect of real cork is desired.	Wash with soap and water; wax.
Vinyl (tile or sheet)	Tough, nonporous, resistant to stains, durable. Comes in clear colors or special effects, including translucent and three-dimensional. The more vinyl content, the higher the price. Comes in great variety of patterns and colors.	Extremely versatile, may be used in any room.	Easy care. Some varieties have built-in lustre and require no waxing.
Cushion-backed Vinyl	Vinyl chips embedded in translucent vinyl base; has pebbly surface; shows no seams; goes on any floor; has cushion backing, making it very resilient.	Wherever desired.	Easy care. Same as other vinyl.
Sheet Vinyl	Lies flat without adhesive.	Wherever vinyl florring is desired.	Same as other vinyl.

**Easily maintained tile is repeated
on wall surface adjacent to range.**
*Courtesy of Armstrong Cork
Company.*

the decorating trend favors exposed hardwood with area or room-size rugs.

Wood may be laid in a variety of ways: in strips, with tongue and groove — a joint in which a projecting member on one side fits into a corresponding groove (1); as planks, uniform or random (2); as parquetry, which makes use of short lengths in various designs, such as checkerboard (3) and herringbone (4) — now assembled at the factory for ease of installation and economy; as prefabricated block, in which plywood or strip flooring is assembled into nine- to twelve-inch squares completely finished in the factory, available for easy installation; as wood veneer, thin layers of wood laminated to a vinyl and asbestos backing to make it durable and more resilient — available in almost any wood, but expensive; maintain as you would vinyl.

Choosing the Right Carpet

Some guidelines regarding color, style, fiber, construction, and size should help make your shopping easier and your final decision a wiser one.

There is today an unprecedented boom in the carpet industry, due in part to the new and improved fibers which have given people carpeting at prices they can afford.

■ Color is usually the first consideration in choosing a carpet — and an important one. Next to the walls, the floor is the largest area of color in the room. The choice should be based on the size of the room, the quantity and quality of light, the amount of traffic, and your own color preference. Colors that are too bright may become tire-

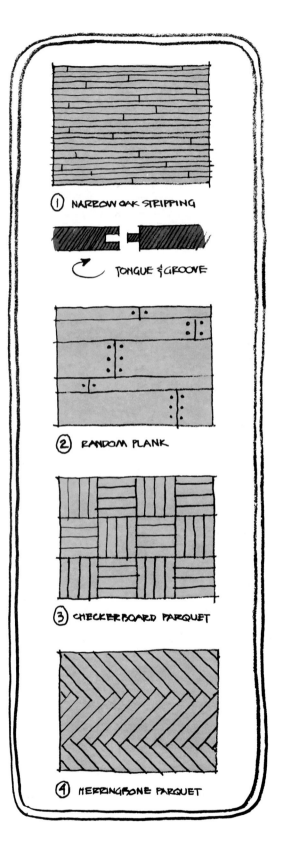

① NARROW OAK STRIPPING

TONGUE & GROOVE

② RANDOM PLANK

③ CHECKERBOARD PARQUET

④ HERRINGBONE PARQUET

Style characteristics of carpet are demonstrated in the samples. Reading from top to bottom: Tip Sheared, Loop Pile, Plush, Embossed, Twist, Shag. *Courtesy of Lees Carpets.*

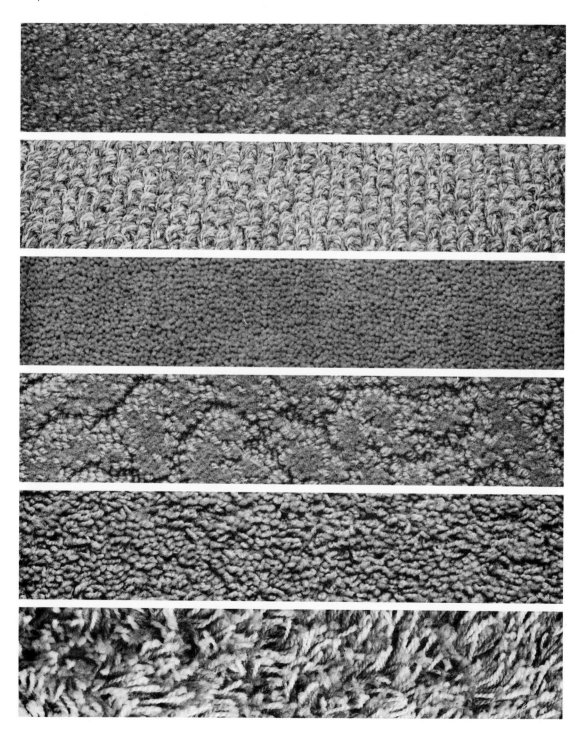

85

some. Medium shades are more practical than very dark or very light ones. If you already have draperies or upholstered furniture, these must be taken into account. Take a sample of the fabric or a pillow or a single drapery with you when you shop for carpet; then take a sample of the carpet home to see it in your own environment. Multitoned combinations are new and have a great youth appeal. But choose a color you feel sure you can live with for a long time.

■ Style, in carpeting, is surface texture and pattern. A *plain* carpet will make your room seem larger than a patterned one, but is the least practical. A *tweed* or a *hard twist* will take hard wear, will hide soil, and will not show footprints. *Embossed* carpets are woven with high and low pile which may be cut, uncut, or a combination of both. These are versatile and more practical than plain. A *shag* will give a feeling of warmth and informality. *Patterned* carpets require a minimum of upkeep but will fill up your room more than plain ones. Keeping in mind the size, use, and general feeling you want in your room, choose from one of the above styles.

Over the years virtually every fiber has been used in carpets, but the field has now been narrowed down to five principal fibers: wool, nylon, acrylic, polyester, and olefin. Each of these has an outstanding quality which accounts for its success, but they all have other supporting qualities.

■ Natural Fibers — *Wool* is the luxury fiber and has long been regarded as the top carpet fiber, possessing all the most desirable characteristics. Other fibers express their aesthetic qualities in terms of how nearly they resemble wool. Wool is resilient; it has warmth, a dull matte look, durability, and soil resistance. It takes colors beautifully, cleans well, and, when cared for, keeps its new look for years. Because of its high cost, wool is not in the top quantity market, but there is no question that it continues its prestigious position in the carpet field. *Cotton* is used mainly for small throw rugs or in areas where traffic is light, since it has a tendency to mat. However, cotton wears and cleans well and holds its color.

■ Man-made fibers — *polyester, acrylic, nylon,* and *olefin* produce carpets that are less expensive than wool. Carpets made from these fibers vary in performance, according to quality of fiber, style, and amount of yarn used, for each fiber lends itself differently to styling and construction. For example, *polyester* is luxurious and feels like wool but mats in shag. *Acrylic* resembles wool and wears and cleans well, but light colors show soil. *Nylon* is the most flexible carpet fiber on the market. It outwears all other carpets and is the least expensive. For these two reasons it accounts for the largest volume of any carpet sold today. However, nylon has a tendency to show soil and does not clean as well as others.

■ Density in carpeting helps to determine wear. Check not only the density but the depth of the pile. In all but shag, bend the sample back to check the density. The less backing you are able to see between the pile, the more dense it is, and hence the longer it will wear. The depth of the pile, easily discerned also, will affect the life of the carpet. Because deeper pile requires more yarn, it will wear longer than a shorter pile. Your dealer will likely indicate density and depth according to the weight.

■ Construction of carpeting is of little concern because over 90 percent of today's carpets are tufted. *Tufting* is based on the sewing machine principle in which threads are inserted into a backing material. To this, a heavy latex coating is applied to anchor the tufts. Many of the patterned carpets that are growing in popularity are woven on the *Axminister* loom, especially where budget price is an important consideration. A recent development is the printed carpet. The method used is basically a screen-printing technique and accounts for an increasing number of fashionably patterned carpets. *Wilton, velvet, needle-punch,* and *knitted* methods account for a very small percentage of carpets made today.

■ The size of your carpet should be determined by your purpose. Wall-to-wall carpeting will expand space, requires only one cleaning process, and gives a maximum of safety. But it cannot be turned for even wear, and only part of it can be salvaged if you move.

A room-size carpet comes within a few inches of the wall, leaving a marginal strip of floor exposed that will need an extra cleaning process. This carpet has most of the advantages of wall-to-wall carpeting plus the benefits that it can be turned for even distribution of wear and may be removed intact.

An area rug is used to define an area of a room according to function. In a one-room apartment when the budget is small, it can help to create a cozy conversation area.

Carpet squares are now available in 12″ squares which may be laid loose and can be interchanged at any time. This type of carpeting is a boon to young people on a meager budget.

Every carpet deserves a good underlay, not only improving the appearance and increasing the resiliency but prolonging the life of the carpet. Even the most moderately priced carpet, laid over a good pad, will take on a feeling of cushioned luxury. Ask your dealer to recommend the best one for your carpet.

About 20 percent of the carpeting sold today has a cushioning already attached. This type of carpet is increasing in popularity and promises to be the answer for Americans on the move, since it can be easily picked up and relaid.

No matter what type of carpet you buy, it should be flameproofed. Check with your dealer about this.

■ To assure getting the best value for your carpet dollar, heed the following three recommendations.

1. Go to a reputable dealer. Always take a sample of the carpet home and live with it. Observe it in the light at different times of the day and under

artificial light. Walk on it. Be sure it is what you want.

2. Buy a dependable brand. Look for a label on the carpet which gives the name of an established manufacturer. This is your assurance of obtaining good value in the price range you select. Also look for the label bearing the generic name which assures you of the fiber content.

3. Choose the best quality your budget will allow. You can always be proud of good quality carpet. It adds beauty and luxury to your home and a world of comfort besides.

Caring for Your Carpet

The amount of care your carpet needs depends upon color, texture, traffic, and the area in which you live. But here are some general rules to follow.

In heavy traffic areas, go over the carpet with a sweeper *once a day.*

Vacuum once a week, except on occasions when the carpet has especially hard use and needs *extra care.*

Professionally clean *once a year* after the first few years. Do not have your carpet cleaned too soon. If it has been cared for and spotted when necessary, complete cleaning ought not to be necessary for several years. However, this depends upon the carpet and the use. Use your judgement.

When spots occur, take *immediate action.* Eliminate stains right after the spill.

1. Blot excess liquid *at once,* working from outside in.

2. Use a soapless powder detergent of low alkalinity. Mix a weak solution of one teaspoon detergent and one teaspoon white vinegar to one quart of warm water. Never use hot water for cleaning carpets.

3. Sponge lightly. *Do not rub or brush.* You can permanently damage the carpet. Avoid getting the back of the carpet wet. It delays drying and may cause mildew.

4. Next, place absorbent material over the damp area and weight it down with books for about six hours.

This procedure is a safe and efficient way to remove stains caused by beverages, washable inks, animal stains, and other water-soluble substances. Other carpet stains usually can be removed by following one of these cleaning methods.

Stains from butter, grease, oil, hand cream, ball-point ink, and hair oil can be removed with a solvent cleaner, such as carbon tetracholoride solution or a commercial home dry-cleaning product. Soak a sponge in the cleaner and blot; don't rub. Follow immediately with absorbent action, using facial tissues or paper towels. Repeat the cleaning process if necessary.

Detergent solutions and solvent cleaners can be used together for the removal of certain stains. For coffee, tea, milk, gravy, egg, sauces, salad dressing, ice cream, and chocolate, sponge the area with detergent solution (several times if necessary) and then apply a solvent cleaner.

For gum, paint, shellac, glue, heavy grease, lipstick, crayon, and candy, apply solvent cleaner first and follow with a detergent solution, using a tissue to absorb excess moisture. Repeat process until the area is clean.

Special stains require special cleaning methods, and if your carpet spot doesn't fall into a general category, call a professional. Consult him also if a stain does not respond to one of the above treatments.

To equalize wear, rotate rugs once or twice a year. On wall-to-wall carpets, try to rearrange your furniture occasionally.

When you carpet a stairway, use a double thickness of padding to lengthen the wear.

WALLS

Rigid Wall Coverings

Walls are a background not only for furniture but for people. Rooms in which people spend little time, such as foyers, may have backgrounds in bold and dramatic patterns, while rooms for relaxing are better if the backgrounds are unobtrusive.

Walls occupy the largest area of a room and serve both functional and beautifying purposes. They are the most important factor in setting the basic theme of the room. Some wall treatments are extremely versatile, while others belong to certain moods and period styles. *Heavy masonry* is most appropriately used in large contemporary rooms and calls for large-scale furniture, heavily textured fabrics, and strong colors. With a current vogue for natural textures, brick and stone are used abundantly both inside and out. *Brick* has been used since the time of the pharoahs and has a timeless quality of warmth and adaptability.

Old brick or brick with the used look is a favorite of many people. *Stone* is less warm then brick, but its durability and strength make it particularly desirable for contemporary rooms, although it is at home in many rooms with a traditional but rustic atmosphere. The *plaster look* is the most versatile of all wall treatments. When plaster is used, different techniques can produce a variety of effects from very rough to very smooth. Because of the high labor costs involved in conventional plaster walls, dry wall (also called sheet rock) has replaced it for most residential use. This comes in $5' \times 7'$ and $5' \times 8'$ sheets, goes on quickly, and, after the seams are filled in, is ready to be painted. A rough plaster effect may be achieved by the application of perfatape compound. Plaster is still used in many commercial buildings. It provides a better insulation and is more fireproof than dry wall. When smooth plaster or dry wall is painted in the right color, it may be used in any room and with any style of furniture. Because of this, the plain wall is the safest background to use in rooms where furnishings may likely be changed from time to time.

There is a new emphasis on *wood paneling* today, but because solid wood planking is costly and requires custom labor, many satisfactory substitutes have been developed. Beautifully grained, factory-finished, and reasonably priced, they are ready for easy installation. *Hardboard and plastic laminate* panels, simulating real wood but impervious to dents, are available at unbelievably low cost and can be easily installed.

Listed in the following chart are the types of rigid wall coverings most commonly used today. Shoppers will find the list helpful in choosing their own wall coverings.

Working Wonders with Wallpaper

No other element of home decoration offers such a wide range of artistic possibilities as wallpaper. It is today's number one all-purpose decorating tool and can revitalize any room. Wall coverings virtually explode with variety, beauty, and practicality. Patterns, styles, and surface effects are unlimited. There are photo murals for one wall or more restrained murals

Rigid Wall Coverings

Masonry

Material	Characteristics	Uses
Plaster and Stucco	Smooth or textured, has no seams or joints. Easy to change. Washable. Insulates against noise.	For any room or any style.
Brick	Durable, appropriate for large or small rooms. Comes in variety of sizes, shapes, colors. Old natural brick has feeling of warmth. Little or no upkeep.	Interior or exterior. Fireplace facing.
Stone	Durable, solid in appearance. Comes in varied shadings of color and texture. May be used in natural shapes or cut for more formality. Little or no upkeep.	Interior or exterior. Fireplace facing.
Cement and Cinder Block	Substantial, cold, generally bold. Best when used in large-scale rooms. Plain or painted.	Interior or exterior. Fireplace facing.
Ceramic Tile	Has desirable aesthetic quality. Comes in variety of shapes, colors, and patterns. Durable, easy to maintain.	Bathrooms, kitchens, utility rooms, dadoes for Spanish and Mexican rooms; becoming more widely used.
Plastic Tile	Excellent do-it-yourself item. Variety of colors. Lightweight. Easy to maintain.	Kitchen, bathrooms, utility rooms.
Metal Tile	Stainless steel: Plain or grained — non-reflective finish. Serviceable, sturdy, not affected by acid, steam, or alkalies. Easy maintenance. Solid copper: Eye appeal. May be plain, hammered, or or antiqued. Sealed to prevent tarnish or corrosion. Aluminum glazes: Solid aluminum coated with a permanent vitreous glaze of porcelain, enamel, or epoxy enamel. Sturdy, easy to maintain.	Wherever sturdy wall covering is desirable. Numerous functional decorative uses. Fireplace, dadoes, bathrooms, kitchens, powder rooms.
Glass Block	Translucent. Permits light into dark area while still maintaining privacy.	Bathrooms, kitchens, foyers in modern homes.

designed to be used continuously on four walls, thus deepening the perspective of a room. There are three-dimensional wall coverings that look like straw matting, bamboo, wood, brick, stone, or marble, to mention only a few. There are papers to add architectural dimension to your room. There are shiny mylars, fancy flocks, practical plastics, and charming prints with fabric to match. Everything from authentic period designs to super graphics are available. They may be expensive, or they may be economical enough for almost any budget. And in spite of their beauty and elegance, these new wallpapers have a practicality never dreamed of a few years ago.

For today's practical decorator, there are numerous flexible wallpapers treated with varying thicknesses of vinyl, made to simulate any type of wall covering, rigid or nonrigid. They may be washable or scrubbable and are waterproof, highly durable, and stain resistant and can be used on nearly any

Paneling

Material	Characteristics	Uses
Solid Wood	Natural grain goes all the way through. Comes in a variety of natural grains from rough barnwood to rich grains for formal rooms. (Can be installed tongue and groove, plain edged, flush joint, or grooved.) Natural colors vary, but may be stained any color. Can be refinished indefinitely. Expensive. Requires little upkeep.	Depending on the type of wood and method of installation, it will go in any room, period or modern.
Plywood	Thin surface of wood veneer is bonded to rugged and inexpensive panel backing. Appearance much the same as solid wood but is less expensive. Comes in sheets 4' × 8' for easy installation. May or may not have vertical grooves.	Wherever wood paneling is desired.
Hardboard — Wallboard (Pressed Wood)	Extremely durable, dent-resistant, low cost, wide variety of wood grains and colors. Wood grain is applied via high-fidelity photo process. Factory coated, virtually indestructible, easily installed. Also available in embossed and textured surfaces simulating fabrics.	In any area where wood paneling of low cost and durability is required.
Plastic Laminate- Wallboard (Pressed Wood)	Extremely durable. Surface of plastic laminate similar to plastic counter top. Photo process of wood grains or solid colors or patterns. Has random grooving if desired, easily installed.	Hard-knock areas of the house, ie., family room, boys' rooms, basements.
Gypsum Wallboard (Plasterboard)	Lowest in cost. Surface is finished in attractive colors and patterns or imprinted with photo-process wood-grain appearance.	Widely used for interior walls where low cost is primary consideration.
Fiber Glass Panels	Translucent panels of reinforced fiberglass. Most often ribbed or corrugated. Also available in flat sheets and in several thicknesses. Comes translucent, white, or colored, and is made to simulate brick, stone, or wood.	Room dividers, folding screens, tub enclosures, translucent lighting panels for ceilings, built-ins, and sliding doors.

type of wall. These vinyl paper or fabric-backed coverings are applied the same as wallpaper, but unlike paper they can be stripped off walls and even reused.

Common Terms

Because wallpaper plays such an important role in today's decorating and because many a homemaker at one time or another will purchase and even try her hand at hanging paper, it is wise for her to be familiar with some of the common terms.

Washable. Usually refers to a wall covering which may be washed with lukewarm, mild suds, but not scrubbed excessively.

Scrubbable. Refers to wall covering which is more resistant to rubbing than the washable types. Stains, such as crayon marks, can generally be removed from scrubbable materials with cleaning agents recommended by the manufacturer or with soap and water.

Pretrimmed. Refers to rolls of wallpaper from which the selvage has been trimmed for your convenience.

(Far left). Enliven rooms with gay scrubbable wall paper. Striped shades with cornice complete the background. *Courtesy of Window Shade Manufacturers Association.*

COLORPLATE 14 (Above). To avoid the stereotyped, add cabinets with washable vinyl. Vibrant blue accents and colorful prints complete the striking room. *Courtesy of Imperial Wallcoverings and Collins and Aikman.* **(Below). Backgrounds needn't be dull. Areas of sharp color contrast with white and create a lively playroom for any age group.** *Courtesy of Evans Products Company.*

93

COLORPLATE 15. For the
sophisticated look, this bathroom
in black slate and natural-grained
wood should be just the thing.
Sharp green and white accents,
a plant or two, and a favorite
print complete this not-run-of-the-
mill room. *Courtesy of Evans
Products Company.*

Semitrimmed. The selvage has been trimmed from one edge only.

Prepasted. Paper has had paste applied during the manufacturing process. Detailed instructions for hanging are usually included. In general, prepasted paper should be soaked in water and applied to the wall while wet.

Single roll. Wallpaper is always priced by the single roll but usually sold by the double or triple roll. Regardless of width, a single roll contains thirty-six square feet.

Double and triple rolls. Regardless of width, a double roll contains 72 square feet and a triple roll contains 108 square feet. Usually 18-inch and 20-inch wallpapers come in double rolls and 28-inch wallpapers come in triple rolls. Double or triple rolls are used to minimize waste when cutting into strips.

Wallpaper As Problem Solver

There is nothing like wallpaper to instantly solve a myriad of decorating problems. It can rescue a dull, shoebox room with sparse and characterless furniture, immediately giving it beauty and glamour. If you want it on all walls, select a pattern that will not "fill up" the room but will supply a pleasant background. If you want only one wall papered, you may use a paper with a larger scaled pattern and more intricate detail. Pick up one of the colors from the paper, neutralize it, lighten it if necessary, and paint the other three walls. Fabrics used in the room should have a minimum of design

and should pick up the colors from the paper.

If your room lacks architectural interest, select a paper that will simulate architectural elements and will enhance your room, such as lattice work, pilasters, or a dado. See the change that occurs.

If your ceiling is too low, it can be psychologically raised by using a striped paper on the wall. If the wall is coved, run the paper onto the ceiling for about one foot. The room will immediately seem to take on added height.

If there is an unsightly jog in the room, a small all-over-patterned wallpaper will conceal it.

Establish a mood with wallpaper. Create a feminine mood in a girl's room by using a delicate floral or stripe. Set a masculine mood in a boy's room with such designs as bold plaids, ships, or animals.

There are many ways in which wallpaper borders can be used to enhance a room. Put one against the ceiling on a plain wall; use one to frame a mirror; cover a free-standing screen with wallpaper, and outline it with a border. These are only a few of the things that can be done to establish or change the atmosphere of a room with wallpaper. Explore its endless possibilities. Watch for special sales. When you buy wallpaper, hang it yourself. For the time and money you spend, nothing you can do will so quickly and completely revitalize tired, uninteresting rooms.

95

Suggestions and Assignments for Part 4: Start with Backgrounds

Suggested Teaching Aids and Procedures

1. Show samples of hard-surface flooring. You may obtain discontinued samples from your local stores.
2. Illustrate different kinds of carpets, showing types of fibers and surface styles. Stress the importance of establishing how an area will be used before choosing a carpet and going to a reputable dealer.
3. Discuss how to care for carpets.
4. A field trip to a carpet store would be helpful. Previous arrangements should be made with a salesman so that he will be prepared to give the students a clear demonstration of carpet construction, fibers, and styles.
5. Illustrate rigid wall coverings and discuss the practical purposes they serve.
6. Have students suggest unique ways of using wallpaper.

Student Assignments

Left to the discretion of the teacher.

COLORPLATE 16. An area rug needn't be square or round. Shape it to suit your fancy and at the same time add pattern to your floor. The blue wall is a striking foil for the white furniture and the graphic. *Courtesy of Armstrong Cork Company.*

5

Fabric Works Magic

COLORPLATE 17. What magic fabric can create! An attic becomes a dream world when fabric is used lavishly on walls, window, and bed. The poofy white spread tied and edged in green adds just the right amount of contrast. An old metal headboard accents the red, and the green rug holds it all together. *Courtesy of Imperial Wallcoverings and Collins and Aikman.*

Think of the most beautiful room you know. Now, visualize this room as we take down the curtains and drapery, remove the carpeting, strip the furniture of its cushions and upholstery, and take away all other fabrics, such as wall coverings, wall hangings, table covers, and screens. Now, what do you see? A room void of warmth, comfort, beauty, mood, and personality. But the architectural features are still there; the furniture is in place. What has made the difference? Fabric!

Since ancient times, it has been recognized that fabric, when skillfully used, is the surest means of creating successful rooms. Never has it been more true than today. And the fabrics need not be costly. Some of the familiar and inexpensive materials that we have seen for years can be used in new and numerous ways, never thought of before. The market abounds in materials that are durable and washable and that fit almost every budget.

Know about Fibers

In order to get the most out of a fabric, you must know what to expect from various fibers. The natural fibers — wool, silk, cotton, and linen — are still available and for many purposes have never been surpassed; but because of shortages and economic problems, the cost has increased so much that fabrics made from natural fibers (with the possible exception of cotton) are beyond the reach of most people.

Natural Fibers

■ Wool is probably the most important natural fiber. It is resilient, durable, dirt resistant and easily cleaned, and it takes and holds any dye. Mohair is a particular type of wool. Wool is used for drapery and upholstery, but particularly for carpeting. However, the soaring price of wool in recent years has limited its use.

■ Silk is the most luxurious and

101

beautiful fiber. It is soft, yet strong and takes and holds dyes. But it deteriorates in sunlight. The cost of silk is high.

■ Cotton is the most plentiful of the natural fibers. It wears well, takes and holds colors, and washes well. It is extremely versatile and may be expensive, but the price varies.

■ Linen is strong and pliable, washes well, and takes and holds colors. It wrinkles unless chemically treated, which treatment then reduces the wear potential. It is particularly good for casements, drapery, upholstery, and slip covers.

To fill the need for quantities of fabric at prices people can afford, many man-made fibers that contain remarkable qualities have been developed.

Man-made Fibers

Man-made fibers fill present-day needs and account for the bulk of decorative fabrics used today. Because manufacturing companies must identify their own products, each fabric is given a trade name. Hundreds of such names exist, and they can be confusing to the consumer. Fortunately, it is not necessary that you know them all. What is necessary is that you know something about the various chemical families.

Each chemical family has a *generic* (family) name, and the Federal Trade Commission requires that this generic name appear on the label of all textiles; it is your assurance of what you are buying. All members of a chemical family have the same characteristics,

(Upper left). Patterned sheets enliven a room at little cost. Vinyl bean bag and mushroom stools take hard use. Carpet stripping adds interest. *Courtesy of Celanese Fibers Marketing Company.*
(Above). Striking fabric against plain backgrounds makes a dramatic statement. Striped shades and colorful rug repeat the colors. *Courtesy of Window Shade Manufacturers Association.*
(Below). Repeat a fabric for dramatic effect. The lively floral feels just right with the wicker furniture. *Courtesy of Window Shade Manufacturers Association.*

varied, of course, by quality and construction. If you know what you can expect from particular families or fibers, you can choose the fabric that is best suited to your needs. So before making a purchase, *read the label.*

Of the man-made fibers developed to date, the most commonly used ones are listed below. New and improved technology has revolutionized production and improved the quality of all man-made fibers. For example, acetate and rayon, the oldest man-made fibers, once considered to be poor cousins, are now among the glamour fabrics. To buy fabrics intelligently, learn all you can about the most common fibers and for what purpose they can best serve you.

■ Acetate drapes well; washing it depends upon construction; it may fade in sunlight; it is the least expensive of man-made fibers. It is used in bedspreads, drapery, and upholstery.

■ Rayon wears well, holds color, resists sunlight, and is inexpensive. It is used for curtains, drapery, and upholstery.

■ Nylon is extremely durable, wears longer than any of the other fibers, is washable and quick-drying, and is inexpensive. It has great versatility and is used for drapery (not sheers, since sunlight deteriorates it), upholstery, and carpeting.

■ Polymide nylon is a chemical fiber with a makeup similar to nylon, but with more versatile properties. It is said to outperform any existing synthetic in washability, wrinkle resistance, and ease of care. It does not shrink. It resembles silk luster, weight, drapability, and color. It may be washed or dry-cleaned and ironed at the same temperature used for cotton. This newest polymide nylon fiber promises to be a most versatile one for many decorative fabrics. It is known by the trade name Qiana (Kee'ana).

■ Acrylic is luxurious, soft, long-wearing, resilient, and quick-drying; and it cleans well. Used for carpeting, it is more like wool than any of the other man-made fibers. It is used also for curtains, drapery, and upholstery.

■ Modacrylic is modified acrylic, with the qualities of acrylic except that it is also flame resistant. Washing is recommended.

■ Polyester is the original drip-dry. It wears well and resists sunlight and mildew. It also resists wrinkling, stretching, and shrinking; and it cleans well. It is used in curtains, drapery, upholstery, pillow floss, and carpeting.

■ Olefin. (polypropylene is a specific type of olefin and the best known) is soil resistant — its most notable characteristic. Used primarily for kitchen and outdoor carpets, it is beginning to be used in upholstery fabrics.

■ Glass fibers are fireproof and impervious to moisture, mildew, sun, and salt air. They are easily washed, quick-drying, and need no ironing. Sewing is a problem since the fibers are hard on hands. They are used principally for curtains and drapery.

■ Vinyl is the general name applied to any group of thermoplastic resins. It is durable, supple, and stain resistant and comes in a wide range of surface

(Left). Against solid-toned walls a striped fabric for upholstery and window shades is carefully coordinated with the bold cushioned vinyl floor. *Courtesy of Armstrong Cork Company.* (Below). Stunning is the word for this room. Clean straight lines and suede-covered furniture are set against a striking carpet. *Courtesy of Thayer Coggin Inc.*

textures and patterns. It is used for shower curtains, upholstery, wall covering, and a myriad of resilient floor coverings.

■ Anidex is the newest generic group. This is a stretch fiber. It is washable, colorfast, and permanently pressed, and has soil-release finishes. It is used for upholstery and slip covers.

Through modern technology and research, new fibers are brought onto the market from time to time. Watch for them. Learn about them. But before you make a major purchase, be sure they have been thoroughly tested.

Solving Problems with Fabric

In addition to giving warmth, beauty, glamour, and personality to your rooms, fabric can solve most of your decorating problems.

Lighten a room. If your room is too dark, paint the walls a warm off-white. Then select a sheer curtain fabric as near the wall color as possible and hang it over the window. The light that filters through will lighten the room and add an airy atmosphere.

Emphasize or conceal objects or architectural features. If you wish to emphasize or make important any element in your room, you can do it with fabric. For example, if your windows are the nice features in your room, make them more important by using a pretty fabric that contrasts with the walls. If, instead, you wish to make the windows inconspicuous, choose a plain fabric in a color closely blended to the walls; they will become surprisingly unnoticeable. Practice this principle in every room of your home.

Set the mood of a room. Through a knowledgeable use of fabric, a drab, colorless room can take on any mood you wish. For example, if you want a cheerful, casual, lived-in look, choose fabrics in lively colors and handcrafted textures. If a formal mood suits you, choose colors that are more neutralized and that have smoother textures (1).

Make a room either feminine or masculine. A feminine mood can be established through the use of fabrics in soft colors, smooth textures, delicate floral patterns, and filmy sheers. A masculine mood can be created through the use of vibrant or deep colors, rough textures, or bold patterns — preferably abstracts or geometrics (2).

Make a room appear larger or smaller. If your problem is one of limited space, select fabric for windows and furniture that blends with the walls, using light colors throughout (13, part 2). Plain or small allover patterns will seem to take up little space. If your problem is that you have small and sparse furniture in a big room, make slip covers out of lively prints. Repeat one of them at the window, and your room will take on a new and well-furnished look.

After you have learned some guidelines, be a bit daring with fabrics. When you know the rules, breaking them seems all right. Remember that it takes a certain sophistication to do the unorthodox thing successfully. But through experience you will find that there is sheer delight in working with

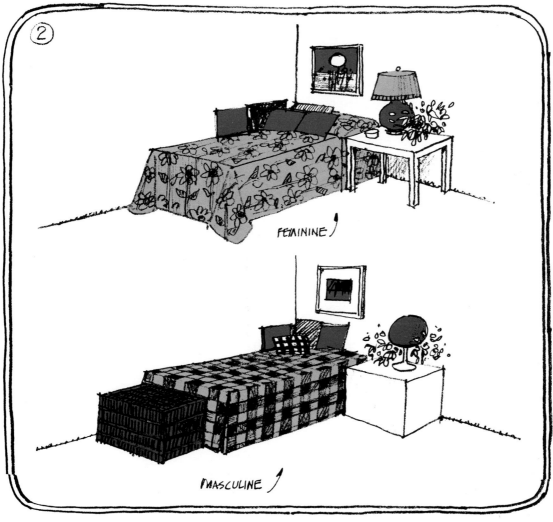

107

fabric and that through this medium, more than any other, the character of your home will be established.

The choice of fabrics today, both plain and patterned, is overwhelming. In plain fabrics you find a vast range of colors and a great variety of textures, and in patterns the selection seems un-limited. With so much at our disposal, it becomes a difficult task for the amateur to make a choice. The most common question asked of professional decorators today is, "What goes with what?" To this question there is no pat answer, but a few guidelines may be helpful.

What Goes With What?

■ Patterns used within the same room must have a pleasing relationship to each other. There should be common elements which tie them together. One or more of the elements, such as color, texture, or motif, throughout the room will give a flow of unity to the entire scheme.

■ The principal pattern need not be repeated in the room, so long as one or more of the colors in that pattern are carried over into another area. A pleasing effect can result from repeating the same pattern on several pieces of furniture, at the windows, and on the furniture — or on the walls, windows and furniture. This is particularly successful in a girl's bedroom. The pattern must be carefully chosen; the final product should not be too busy, too stimulating, or overpowering.

■ A room should have no more than one bold pattern of the same design, such as a floral, except in very rare cases. Once the dominant motif is established, it may be supplemented by a small pattern, a stripe, a check or a plaid, with appropriate textures if there is a common denominator throughout.

"OH, NANCY, I'M HOME! NANCY! WHERE ARE YOU?"

■ When combining patterned fabrics, scale and proportion must be carefully considered. For example, bold, informal floral patterns call for bold plaids and strips as "roommates," while more formal floral designs require more delicate and refined coordinates.

■ Not only pattern but texture must also be considered in combining fabrics. As a general rule, rough, informal textures such as tweed, corduroy, ticking, burlap, canvas, and muslin go well together, while more formal fabrics with smoother surfaces such as velvet, damask, and satin are compatible. But no hard and fast rule exists about combining textures. Don't think you must always cling to the conventional way. Try new and fresh ways of using and combining both pattern and texture. An unexpected combination of textures can be exciting. For example, try edging heavy unbleached muslin drapery with velvet. Another idea is to use vinyl welting in a glazed chintz slip cover.

Don't be afraid to try fabric on the wall. It has been done for hundreds of years, and today it is high fashion and good taste if the fabric is appropriate. Begin by doing only one wall of a small room where, if the result is something less than perfection, it will not be disastrous. Burlap, felt, faded blue denim, and ticking are some good choices to begin with. There are a number of ways of applying fabric to walls, but perhaps the best is the paste method. A coat of modocol is first applied to the wall and allowed to stand. When the fabric is ready to be applied, paint a second coat of modocol and apply the fabric as you would wallpaper. You will be amazed to see a nondescript room transformed.

109

Suggestions and Assignments for Part 5: Fabric Works Magic

Suggested Teaching Aids and Procedures

1. Discuss the common fibers — natural and man-made. Suggest which fibers are the best for specific purposes.
2. Show illustrations of how fabric can solve decorating problems.
3. Have some large pieces of fabric and demonstrate ways of coordinating pattern and texture.

Student Assignments

Coordinate colors and fabrics to complete work sheets 7 and 8.

Work Sheets 7 and 8

Objective

The objective of these projects is to give the student an opportunity to demonstrate his or her ability to create a definite mood through the appropriate use of fabrics. Special attention must be given to color, texture, and pattern in coordinating the fabrics to establish the desired mood.

Instructions to Students

1. Carefully examine the example showing a completed room.
2. Work sheet 7: By selecting the appropriate colors, patterns, and textures, create in this room an *informal* mood.
3. Work sheet 8: By selecting the appropriate colors, patterns, and textures create in this room a formal mood.

WORK SHEET #7

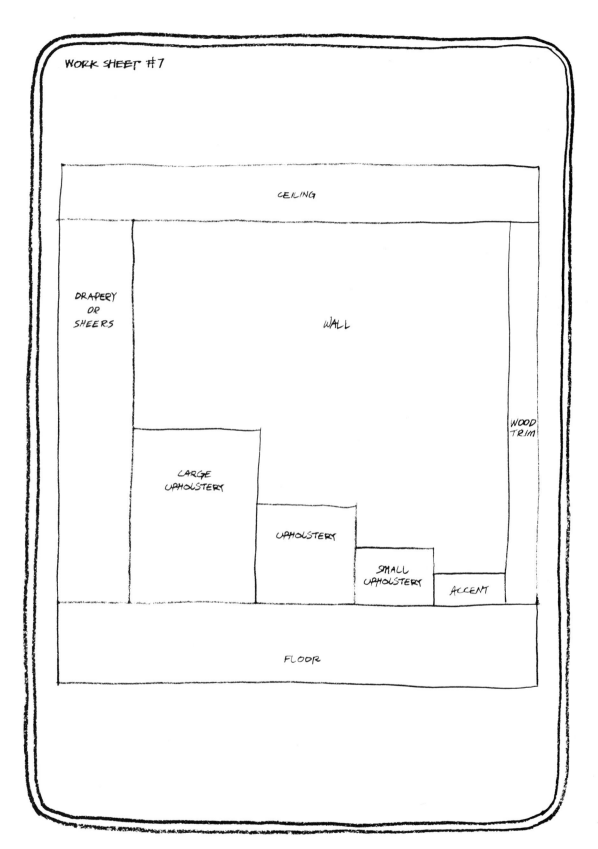

CEILING

DRAPERY
OR
SHEERS

WALL

WOOD
TRIM

LARGE
UPHOLSTERY

UPHOLSTERY

SMALL
UPHOLSTERY

ACCENT

FLOOR

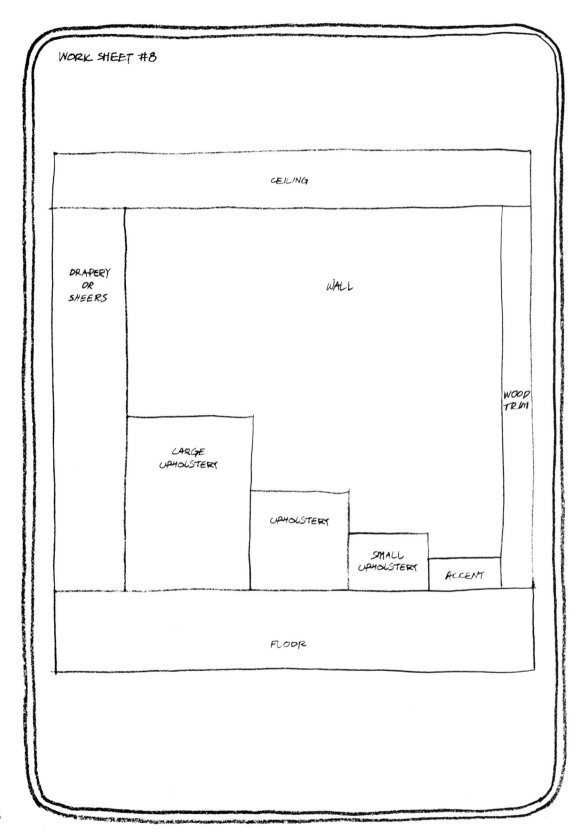

WORK SHEET #8

CEILING

DRAPERY OR SHEERS

WALL

WOOD TRIM

LARGE UPHOLSTERY

UPHOLSTERY

SMALL UPHOLSTERY

ACCENT

FLOOR

112

COLORPLATE 18. Well coordinated fabrics create a variety of moods. (Upper left). A striking red, black and white room. White walls and black shutters, with a red carpet of cut and uncut pile, make up the background against which a heavy, cotton stylized print, coordinated stripe, red suede, black patent vinyl, and white fake fur create a lively scheme for a boy's bedroom. (Upper right). A two-color scheme for the lover of green and blue. The colors here are taken from the carpet. Compatible textures of heavy cotton, wide corduroy, fake fur, and patent vinyl against white walls create a dramatic yet liveable room. (Left). A stripe picks up most of the colors of the print, green cotton damask, plain apricot twill, and dark vinyl pull out some of the other colors. Warm, off-white semisheers and soft, apricot carpet complete the room. 113

6

No Window Problems

COLORPLATE 19. Everyone
loves a window nook. And what
could be more pleasant than the
one featured here? High-back
settees, soft furry rug for bare feet,
light for reading, and shelves
and drawers for storage. Carved
window frame, appliqued blind,
and frothy cafe curtain complete
the feminine retreat. *Courtesy of
Armstrong Cork Company.*

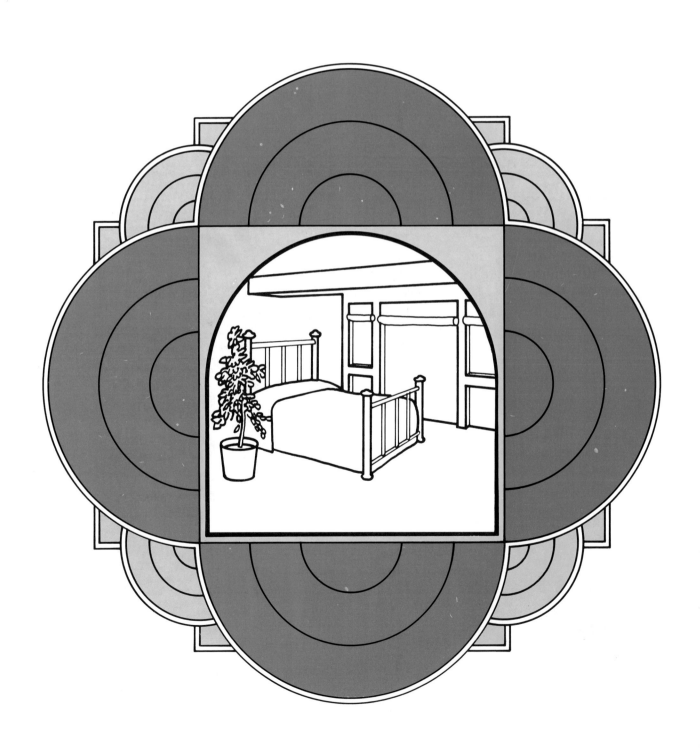

Your windows are one of the most important features of your entire decorative scheme. A well-planned window treatment can make up for the lack of insufficient furniture in a room; it can set the color scheme or the overall mood and can add beauty and glamour. So never take a window lightly!

Learn About Windows

Any window treatment must begin with a plan. Decide upon the overall effect you want in your room; then make your window an important feature in that plan.

Basic Types of Windows

A good place to begin is by learning the basic types of windows and their most common treatments. Listed below are the most commonly used ones with accompanying sketches and suggested treatments.

The window is a conspicuous element in both the exterior and interior design of the house. As a source of interior light, it is the first point to which the eye is drawn during the daytime; at night a lighted window is the first thing seen from the outside. The treatment of a window is determined by the style of architecture, the type and size of the window, the exposure, the placement in the wall, and the furnishings of the room. With modern architecture new types of window openings have been introduced. Many types of windows unknown only a few decades ago are now as familiar as the standard casement or double-hung type. Windows that once were a problem are a problem no longer, thanks to the new freedom in window decoration. Whatever your window, simply visualize it as you would like it to look, then proceed to make it look that way. Begin by learning about windows.

117

- Double-hung: Made up of two sashes which may be raised and lowered (1).
- In-swinging casements: Curtains and draperies must be hung in such a way as not to tangle with the window (2).
- Ranch windows: Usually wide-set high in the wall. Most often used in ranch-type or contemporary houses (3).
- Bay windows: Either bowed or angled. These windows have great possibilities (4).
- Picture windows: Have a large pane of glass or a fixed pane with movable side sections (5).
- Corner windows: Two windows come together at a corner (6).
- Slanting and clerestory windows: Follow the line of a slanting roof. These may be treated in a variety of ways (7).
- Jalousie windows: Have wide horizontal sashes that open outward to any angle (8).
- French doors: Usually come in pairs. The problem here is similar to the in-swinging casement (9).
- Dormer windows: Project from an alcove in the roof and usually fill up the entire space, thus presenting a decorating problem, since they need to be opened to admit air (10).

Other types of windows are not so frequently used. Your hardware store can likely furnish you with a brochure illustrating these.

Window Terminology

A knowledge of window and hardware terminology will simplify purchasing and measuring. (See illustration on following page.)
- The *casing* is that part of the window that fits into the wall structure.

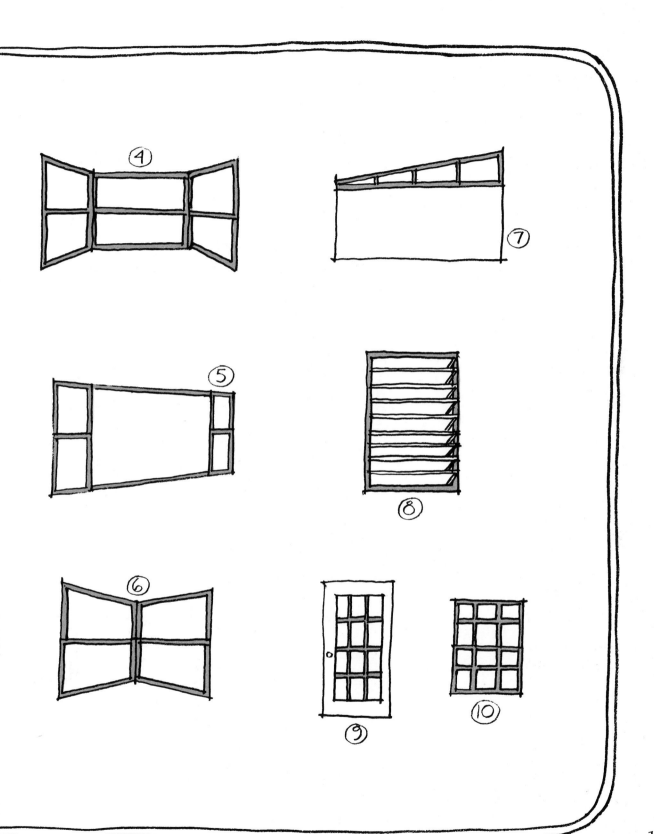

119

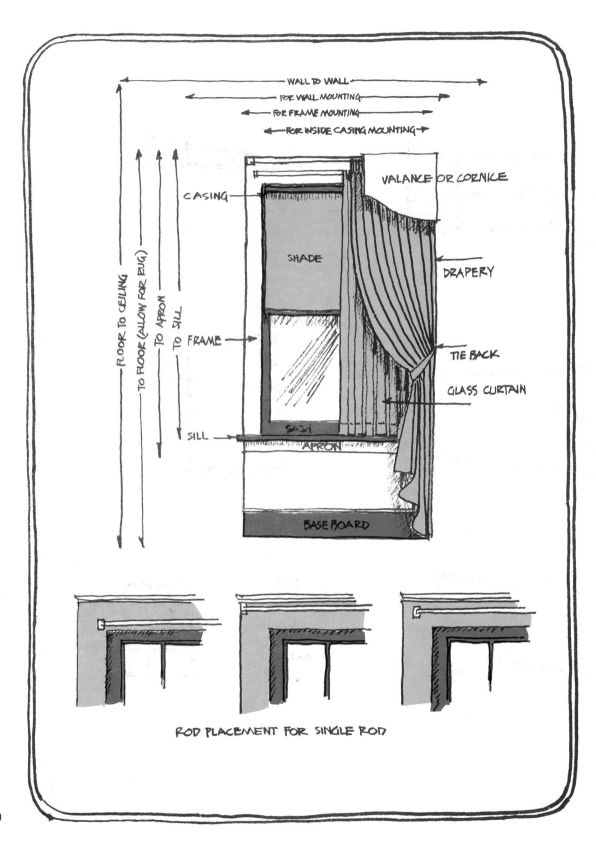

WALL TO WALL

FOR WALL MOUNTING

FOR FRAME MOUNTING

FOR INSIDE CASING MOUNTING

FLOOR TO CEILING

TO FLOOR (ALLOW FOR RUG)

TO APRON

TO SILL

CASING

SHADE

FRAME

SILL

SASH

APRON

BASE BOARD

VALANCE OR CORNICE

DRAPERY

TIE BACK

GLASS CURTAIN

ROD PLACEMENT FOR SINGLE ROD

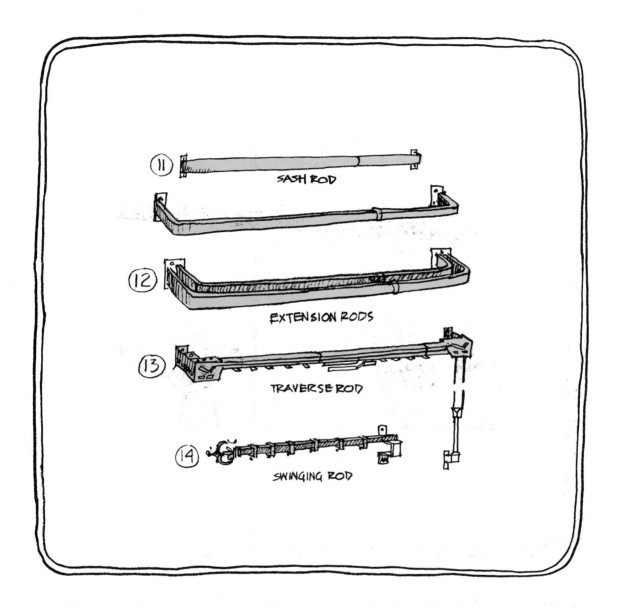

The *frame* is the wide molding which covers the casing and frames the glass.
- The *sash* is the part that holds the glass.
- The *sill* is the narrow shelf at the bottom of the sash.
- The *apron* is the part of the frame below the sill.
- A *sash rod* is a flat rod attached close to the sash, both top and bottom, on which curtains are shirred. These are most often used to cover the glass of inswinging doors and casements (11).
- *Extension rods* are single and double; they are used for curtains and stationary drapery (12).
- *Traverse rods* operate on a pulley system. They may be one-way or two-way and are used to draw casements or drapery over the window (13).
- *Swinging rods* allow for stationary drapery to be swung back. Suitable for in-swinging casements, French doors, and dormer windows (14).

121

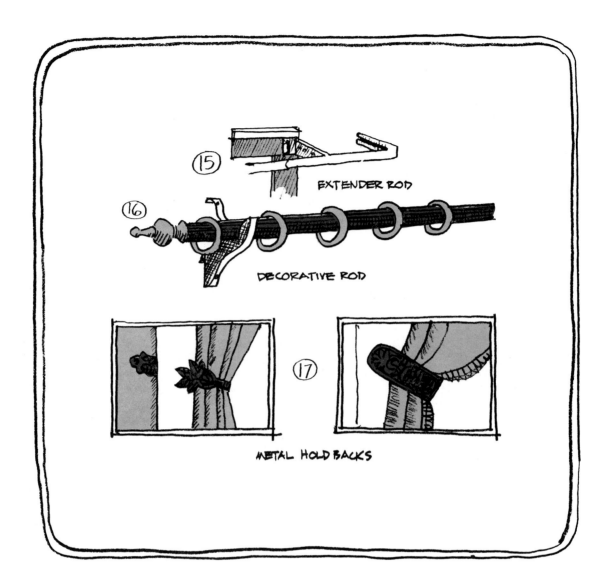

EXTENDER ROD (15)

DECORATIVE ROD (16)

(17)

METAL HOLD BACKS

■ *Extender rods* extend and hold stationary drapery (15).

■ *Decorative rods* are used for stationary or draw drapery. In measuring for drapery here, there is no return (16).

■ *Metal hold-backs* are used to hold drapery back on one or both sides (17).

These are the simplest kinds of curtain rods. No matter what your window problem, a rod is available to handle it. Your sales person will refer you to brochures with complete information as to the kind of rod you need in any circumstance.

Types of Window Hangings

Learn the following types of window hangings, the qualities each should have in order to perform efficiently, and some decorative treatments.

■ Glass curtains or sheers are hung permanently against the glass and must

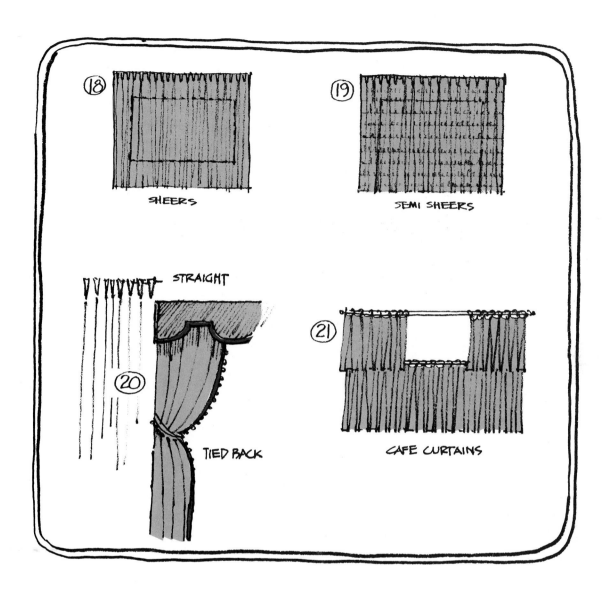

SHEERS

SEMI SHEERS

STRAIGHT

TIED BACK

CAFE CURTAINS

be sheer, sunproof to color fastness and splitting, and washable without shrinkage; most often they are off-white (18).

■ Semi-sheers are drawn over the window for privacy. They are usually neutral in color and must be sun resistant to splitting and washable or cleanable without shrinkage (19). They have a luxurious look.

■ Side draperies may be stationary, either hanging straight or tied back, only at the sides of the window for

beauty; or they may be drawn for nighttime privacy. The fabric must be drapable and should clean without shrinkage (20).

■ Cafe curtains are any curtains hung from a rod by rings or loops over the lower part of a window, usually for privacy (21).

■ Window shades are usually hung on the inside of the window frame to be drawn for nighttime privacy. They may be purely functional or decorative as well. The material is varied.

123

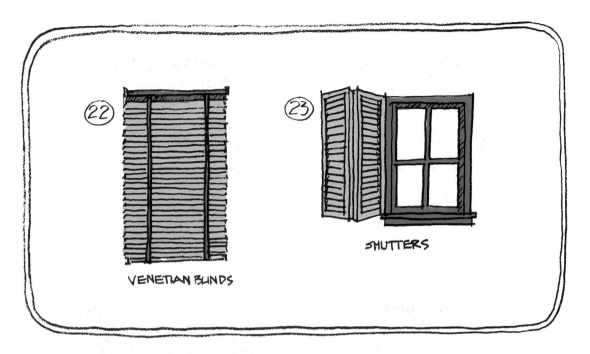

VENETIAN BLINDS

SHUTTERS

- Venetian blinds are made of adjustable horizontal slats used instead of window shades to control the light. They are available in metal or plastic and are very durable (22).
- Shutters are made of horizontal slats that fit inside a frame. They are attached to the window casing and may fold back to become a unified part of the room, substituting for drapery (23).
- Valances are horizontal drapery treatments that go across the top of the window over the drapery. They may be pleated or shaped (24).
- Swags are a graceful window treatment devised to drape material over the top of the window and taper to the corners (25).
- Jabots drape down from the corners of the swag. They are usually pleated and may be of varying lengths (25).
- Cornices are usually box-like horizontal treatments that go across the top of the window over the drapery. They may be painted or covered with

fabric or other decorative material (26).
- Tie backs are used to hold drapery back. They may be cords with tassels or made of fabric (27).

When hanging curtains and draperies, the bottom should come to one of three points: *to the sill, to the bottom of the apron,* or *to the floor — nowhere between.*

Rods may be attached at a number of points: within the window frame if curtains are to come to the sill, on the upper and outer corners of the frame, on the wall near the ceiling — to make the room appear higher — or on the wall to the side of the window, giving the illusion of a wider window.

Procedure for Measuring a Window and Estimating Yardage

To determine the length of the curtain

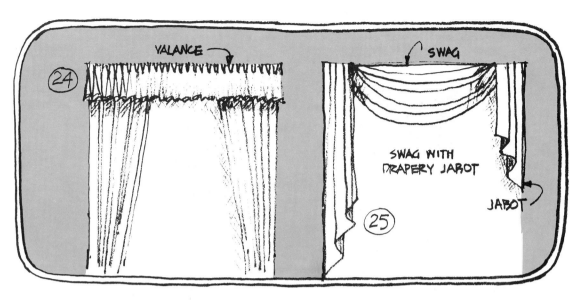

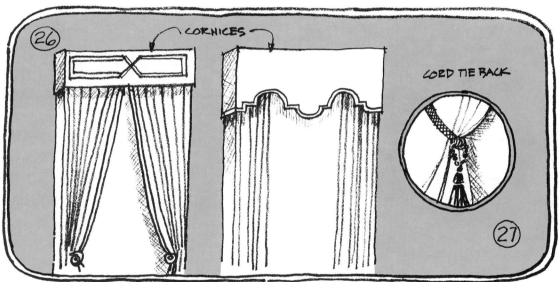

125

or drapery, follow these steps:

1. Measure from top of the rod to the desired length. This will give you the *finished* length.

2. Add 12 inches to the finished length to allow for 5 inches at the top and a double 3 1/2-inch hem at the bottom. This will give you the *cutting* length.

To determine the width and the number of fabric lengths necessary, follow the steps listed below:

1. Measure the length of the face of the rod.

2. Add twice the length of the *return*. (The return is the distance from the face of the rod to the wall or window casing where the brackets fastens.)

3. Add 6 inches for *overlaps*. (When drawn drapery come together in the middle, one panel should lap over the other about 3 inches to prevent a gap and to insure privacy. This is called the *overlap*.)

4. Allow 1 1/2 inches to 2 inches for side hems.

5. Add the amount of drapery estimated in the above steps 1, 2, 3, and 4 together; multiply this amount by two to give double fullness. This will give you the width of material necessary for your window.

The beauty and success of your window treatment depend largely upon the fullness and beauty of the folds; so don't skimp.

6. Measure width of the drapery fabric to determine the number of widths you will need.

An example: The cutting length measures 8 feet (8'). (The sign ' stands

for feet and " stands for inches.)

Rod measures	5'	=	5'
Return measures	2" multiply by 2 =		4"
Overlap measures	3" multiply by 2 =		6"
Side hems measure	2" multiply by 2 =		4"
	Total		6'2"

Double the total amount to allow for fullness: $2 \times 6'2'' = 12'4''$.

Now measure your drapery fabric. Say it is 48" or 4' wide. You need a width of 12'4". Twelve feet divided by 4' = 3 plus 4". You will need 3 lengths of drapery for your window. Disregard the 4" since this small amount can be allowed in the pleating. Measurements rarely come out exactly right. If more than 9" to 12" are left over, you may wish to add another one-half length of fabric. You must use your own judgement depending upon the width of the fabric and the width of the window.

To determine the amount of yardage, multiply the cutting length, which is 8', by 3, which is the number of fabric lengths needed. You will need 8 yards of plain drapery material (8' × 3 = 24'; 24' ÷ 3' = 8 yards).

In estimating for sheers, follow the same procedure, *except* that for fullness, multiply by three instead of two to give triple fullness.

Always recheck your measurements carefully before purchasing and cutting the material. (See below the procedure for making unlined drapery.)

Selecting the Fabric

Fortified with an overall plan for the room, some basic information, and the

(Above). Cotton seersucker is used behind bamboo moldings on doors and windows to define study space and to cover a mattress pad to make the comforter. Parsons table doubles as desk and dressing table. *Courtesy of Celanese Fibers Marketing Company.* (Below). One of many helpful brochures available to help you stretch your decorating dollar. *Courtesy of Window Shade Manufacturers Association.*

knowledge of the principles of design, you are ready to use your own creativity and imagination in transforming the windows in your room into personalized mood-setters. Look carefully at the window you are going to decorate and answer the following questions before you proceed. What purpose does the window serve? Does it give both light and air? Does it have a view worth emphasizing or one to be hidden? Does it allow too much light into the room or not enough? Does it face the street or the garden? How is it located in the wall space? Is it too tall and narrow, too square, or well proportioned? All of these questions must be resolved in your planning. If the window seems right for the completed room you have in mind, consider the basic treatments and select the one that best fits your need. If your window does *not* seem right, visualize it as you would like it to look and *find out* how to make it look that way.

And how does one go about this task? Study pictures of windows that you like until you find one that suits your purpose. Make a picture or a rough sketch of what you have in mind and ask at a drapery department for some practical help on how your idea can be implemented. When the mechanics have been settled, you have come to the enjoyable part — that of selecting the fabric.

The first thing to remember in selecting the fabric is that windows look two ways: to the inside, and to the outside. Many more people will see them from the outside than from the inside; so consider both. Another point to keep in mind is that windows facing the street should appear as much the same from the outside as possible, and all ought to be unobtrusive (28). Patterned fabrics must be lined. Both lining and sheers should be off-white.

Selecting the fabrics that will be right for the windows in your rooms is a very personal thing, and cost is not the most important consideration. Fabrics do not have to be expensive; it is far better to have lavish folds of an inexpensive drapery than skimpy, expensive ones. Never before has there been such a variety of fabrics in all price ranges from which to choose. Materials such as gingham, ticking, muslin, burlap, and canvas can be used with success in an infinite number of ways. Sheets, too, are a great boon to the budget minded and have a myriad of uses other than for drapery. Don't overlook ready-made curtains and drapery; often they can be timesaving and money saving as well as satisfactory for the purpose.

Decorating windows does not have to mean using only fabrics. Window shades today are out in front, not just behind, draperies as they once were. Things to be done with window shades are unlimited. Be imaginative and creative. Paint them, laminate them, or appliqué them. Fasten decorative pull-down shades directly to the window sash and paint the window frame, or hang them on the outside of the frame and see the windows disappear when shades are drawn. All kinds of trim and accessories are available, such

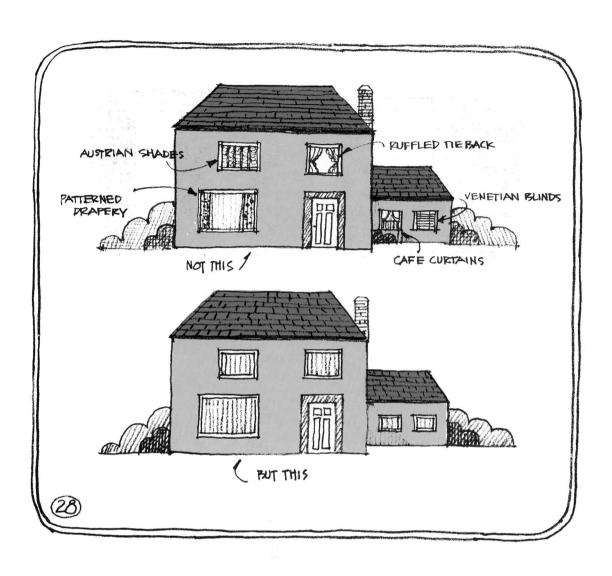

AUSTRIAN SHADES

RUFFLED TIE BACK

PATTERNED DRAPERY

VENETIAN BLINDS

NOT THIS

CAFE CURTAINS

BUT THIS

28

129

as braids; plain, tasselled, and ball trims; and loop fringe, to give that personalized touch. Some variations of window shades are the Roman shade, the minislated blind, and the old standby — the Venetian blind.

Same Window — Different Look

The ideas presented in the accompanying descriptions and illustrations may be helpful in finding solutions to your particular window problem. In each case, you will note how the different treatments of the same window create distinctly different moods.

Take a tall, old-fashioned window and hang full draperies on the wall to just cover the frame, leaving all glass exposed. Attach a valance or cornice to the frame across the top and notice that the window seems lower and wider (29). Drapery may be carried out on the wall to any distance, so long as it looks right in the room.

Take a nearly square window in your room that needs help. Hang sheers from ceiling to floor. If drapery is used, partially cover the glass. The result will be an illusion of a high and important window. A visually raised ceiling will be an extra bonus (30).

Take two side-by-side windows. The variety of ways in which they can be treated is unlimited. Below are three suggested methods.
- Frame them in a wall covered with latticed wallpaper to visually expand space. Hang cotton tie backs over white sheers. Cover a love seat between the windows with white canvas and use a green vinyl welting (31).
- Make a window frame by gluing off-white canvas to heavy buckrum or plywood. Place printed fabric shades on rollers in metal brackets behind the frame. The illusion is that there are

COLORPLATE 20. When framing a garden, some windows need no inside drapery — only a simple blind for nighttime privacy.
Courtesy of Armstrong Cork Company.

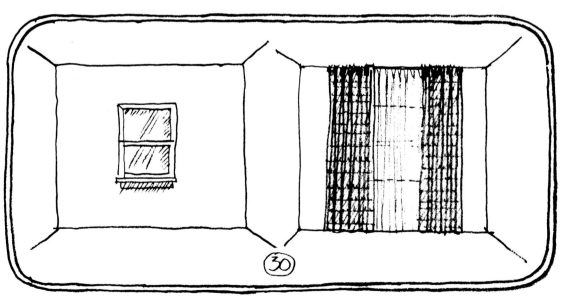

COLORPLATE 21. **Ready-made draperies coordinated with a blind made from a sheet unify a young girl's room.** *Courtesy of Celanese Corporation.*

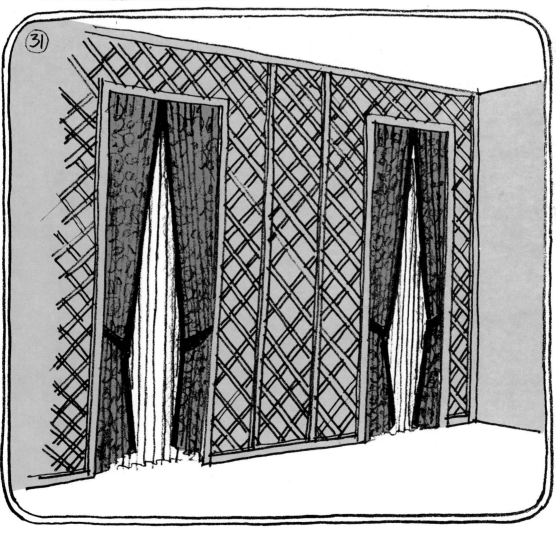

134

three tall windows. The middle shade can conceal storage (32).

■ Create the illusion of a window wall with the two windows. Hang white sheers from floor to ceiling over the entire wall. Cover four hinged do-it-yourself screens with a lively print and place on either side of the two windows. Or cover the screens with ticking and hang bright shades in the three spaces between (33).

There is no limit to how many ways the wall with two windows can be treated. Do whatever pleases you and feels right for your room.

Never underestimate the importance of your windows and what they can do for your rooms. No feature in your room can more quickly catch the eye or set the mood. You can do anything with a window from merely framing the glass to creating a focal point of beauty and glamour. And no matter what new fashion or fad comes along, window treatments that reflect an understanding of good taste will always look right.

How to Make Your Own Curtains and Drapery

Learning how to make your own drapery will save you money now and later on, and the skill you acquire could prepare you for future employment.

Draperies unlined, lined, or both lined and interlined

■ *Unlined drapery.* Many draperies do not need to be lined. Many fabrics in neutral colors, in plain or novelty weaves, hold up under sunlight, permit some light to filter through, are unobtrusive from outside, and provide a variety of effects in the room. Some colored and patterned chintzes are enhanced by back lighting and hence are more attractive without lining. These, however, must be hung at windows looking away from the street. (The procedure for making unlined drapery is adapted from "How to Make your Windows Beautiful" with permission of Kirsch.)

■ *Lined drapery.* Where fragile fabric needs protection from the sun, where light filtering through the fabric destroys the decorative effect, or where you wish a more formal look in the folds, it is advisable to line the drapery. This is not a difficult task. Sometimes the lining is hung separately but on the same rod, and the hooks are attached to the same rings as the drapery. The advantage here is that the lining, which collects soil more quickly than the drapery, can be cleaned separately.

■ *Interlined drapery.* When fabric needs to be protected from the sun and when there is a desire to give an especially heavy and elegant look with deep rich folds of beautiful fabric, an interlining of a flannel-like fabric is placed between the lining and the drapery fabric.

Today probably more unlined draperies are used than lined ones. If you learn how to make the unlined drapery, you can easily learn the techniques of lining later on.

135

The procedure for making unlined draperies is as follows:

1. Install the rods. Take careful measurements. (See above procedure for measuring.)

2. If you choose a patterned material, you must allow for matching the pattern. (Your salesperson will estimate the extra amount of fabric it will take for "repeats" — the matching of the pattern.) Where panels are stitched together, the pattern must match (34); each pair of panels must match; and where the pattern is conspicuous, all draperies in the room should match.

3. When you buy the fabric, also get thread, drapery hooks, and buckram. (Four-inch buckram is standard although five-inch may be used in extra long drapery.) Cut off all selvage edges of drapery fabric to prevent puckering in washing or drycleaning.

4. Lay fabric on a flat surface to cut the panels. Be careful in matching the design in patterned material.

5. If it is necessary to join two lengths of fabric together to get the needed width, use interlocking fell seam:

(a) Place two pieces of material one on top of the other, right sides together. Allow the edge of the lower piece to extend 1/2" beyond the upper piece (35).

(b) Fold the lower edge over the upper edge. Press this fold in place (36).

(c) Make another fold, this time of both pieces. Pin, press, and stitch. This will make a professional-looking seam (37).

6. Cut buckram for the heading. This should be the width of the drapery *less* the side hems. Place the buckram on the wrong side of the fabric 1" from the top. Turn the 1" of fabric over the buckram and stitch the top and the lower edge (38). Fold the 4" of buckram and fabric on the wrong side. The side hems are now ready to be folded.

7. Fold the side hems over the buckram. Make a 1" fold and press. Make a second 1" fold. Press, baste or pin. Stitch by hand, using a blind stitch, or on a machine, using a long, loose stitch (39).

8. Hem the bottom. Turn up 3 1/2" and press. Turn a second time to form a double 3 1/2" hem. Press, baste or pin. Sew on a machine with a long stitch or by hand, using a loose blind stitch (40). (Recheck the *finished* length before turning the bottom hem.)

To make pinch pleat headings

For the nonprofessional, a 4" space between pleats is the easiest to use and makes ample fullness. The space between pleats should remain constant. Make necessary adjustments within the pleats. Be sure to pin the pleats before stitching.

▪ Measure the width of your hemmed panel, subtract overlap and rod returns, and you have the drapery width to be divided into 4" units. Example: say the finished panel is 44", the overlap is 3", and return is 3" Subtract 6 from 44, and your working number is 38. Divide this by 8 (ideally 4" per pleat, 4" per space) and the whole number at which you arrive is 4

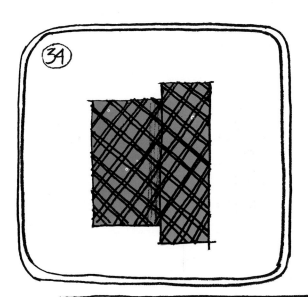

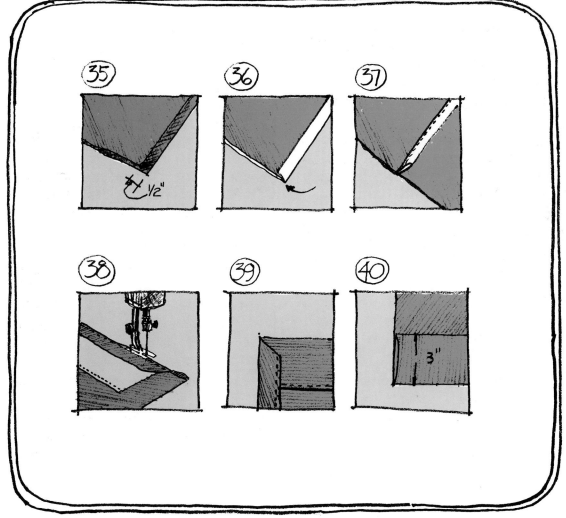

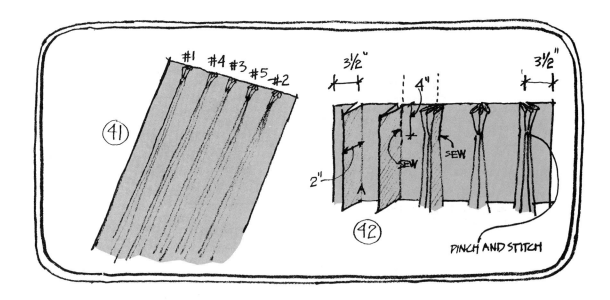

(disregard fractions). This will be the number of *spaces* you can have. The next highest number, 5, will be the number of *pleats* you can have. Now multiply the 4 spaces by 4", and you get 16". Subtract this from 38", to arrive at 22", the amount of fabric you have for making 5 pleats; you can use just a bit over 4" within each pleat. Adapt this formula to your measurements.

■ Starting at the left side of the panel, 3" from the edge, pin pleat #1. Now pin in pleat from #2 at the right side of the panel, 3" from that edge. Next, bring pleats #1 and #2 together to get center pleat #3. Place pleats #3 and #1 together to get #4, and so on (41).

■ Stitch each pleat fold from the top to the bottom of the buckram. Gather each fold into a cluster of three small pleats at the base, and, by hand, sew back and forth, as shown. Extend the small pleats to the top by finger-creasing; then tack them again at the top back edge (42).

■ To create professional looking folds:

after your draperies are hung and pulled back to the sides, start at the top of the drapery and finger each pleat down about a foot or so, "sharpening" the pleats with firm pressure as you go.

■ Tie each panel in position with cotton tape or heavy cording, not too tightly. Continue; tie every foot or so. Leave them for two or three days; untie, and draperies will hang in lovely folds — just like the professionally hung ones!

Easypleat headings

Pleating draperies can be made easier with Easypleat tape. The result will look almost professional, and cleaning and pressing will be simplified because when the hooks are removed, the fabric will lie flat.

The procedure for this method is as follows:

■ Measure the windows, install the rods; also buy Easypleat tape and hooks. Allow two times the length of the rod face plus, for each window, 1/2 yard extra for returns, overlaps, and adjustments.

138

■ Determine the exact width of the fabric you will need by hookpleating your tape before buying the fabric. Allow 4″ on the inside end of the tape for overlap (turn under) at the center of the draperies. Starting at this point, 4″ from the end, pleat the tape for one side (43).

■ Insert prongs of hook in each of four pockets; skip one pocket; repeat. Hang on rod for "fit," starting at the center. In measuring the length, make only 1/2″ allowance for top turn (44).

■ Cut the panels and hem their sides and bottom. Now with drapery right side up, place Easypleat across top edge, covering the top 1/2″ of goods. Pocket openings should point up, with tape overhanging 1/2″ at each side. Pin and stitch (45).

■ Turn drapery panel over; fold back tape to lie against the wrong side of the fabric. Fold under 1/2″ at each end; sew. Stitch along the bottom edge below the pockets you will use to form the pleats with the Easypleat hooks. Insert the hooks (46).

(For more information on making lined draperies, cafe curtains, swags, and jabots, booklets are available that give full instructions. Inquire of the salesperson in the drapery department.

When you hang the draperies you have made, you will find genuine satisfaction and pride in seeing your room take on a new dimension.

As your drapery-making skill and your knowledge of design and the use of color and fabric increase, you may wish to start a drapery business of your own. Your home is a good place to begin, wherever you live. You can set up a workshop in the corner of a room or in the garage, with little or no investment. The skilled drapery craftsman is always in demand in every part of the country. So it is a profession you can take with you anywhere. And if you maintain a high standard of craftsmanship and are dependable, you can be sure of an income until you retire.   139

Suggestions and Assignments for Part 6: No Window Problems

Suggested Teaching Aids and Procedures

1. Discuss basic window types and window terminology.
2. Sketch a window on the blackboard and, with the class, go through the procedure of measuring and estimating yardage.
3. Demonstrate the procedure of making unlined drapery, using plain material. Demonstrate both pinch pleat and Easypleat headings.
4. Explain the problem involved in matching a pattern (repeats). Bring to class two pieces of patterned fabric: one with a small allover pattern, and one with a large pattern.
5. Bring to class a length of completed drapery.
6. Make sketches on the blackboard and show pictures of a number of ways in which either a single window or two windows may be treated.

Student Assignments

1. Estimate the total cost for drapery and sheers for the window on work sheet 9.
2. Show three ways of treating the window on work sheet 10.

3. If time permits, measure, purchase the fabric, and make a pair of draperies for your own room.

Instructions for Work Sheets 9 and 10

Objective

The objective of work sheet 9 is to give the student an exercise in measuring and estimating yardage and cost of curtains and drapery and to acquaint him with labor costs involved.

The objective of work sheet 10 is to encourage the student to use his imagination in solving window problems.

Instruction to Students

Using the dimensions indicated on the sketch, estimate the amount of yardage necessary for sheers and drapery for the window on work sheet 9.

When you have estimated the yardage, determine the total cost using the following criteria: drapery at $3.75 per yard; sheers at $2.50 per yard; drapery hooks at 50c per dozen. For cost of drapery rods, check with your local store. Also check with your local store for labor costs for making unlined drapery and sheers. Add this into your total costs.

Work sheet 10: Make three sketches, showing in each one a different treatment for the window pictured here.

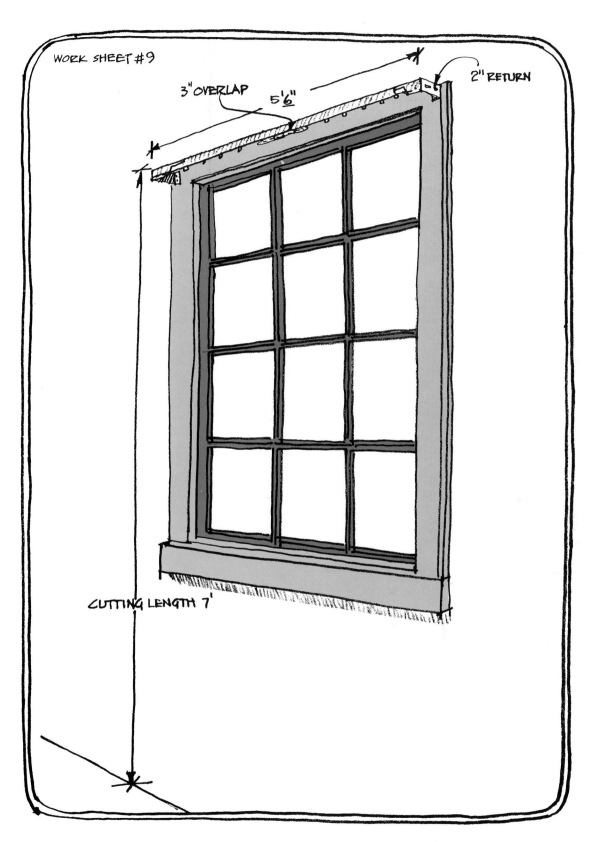

WORK SHEET #9

3" OVERLAP

5' 6"

2" RETURN

CUTTING LENGTH 7'

141

WORK SHEET #10

142

NAME _____

COLORPLATE 22. A window in an unusual place allows added light to the U-shaped kitchen. Fabric-covered table adds a touch of glamour. *Courtesy of Armstrong Cork Company.*

7

Fun with Furniture

COLORPLATE 23. What could be more fun than this red and white room? The handsome tile floor is easy to maintain. Twisted columns and railing mark off the eating area. Unobstructed windows frame the outdoor window boxes, and hanging plants bring more of the outside in. *Courtesy of Armstrong Cork Company.*

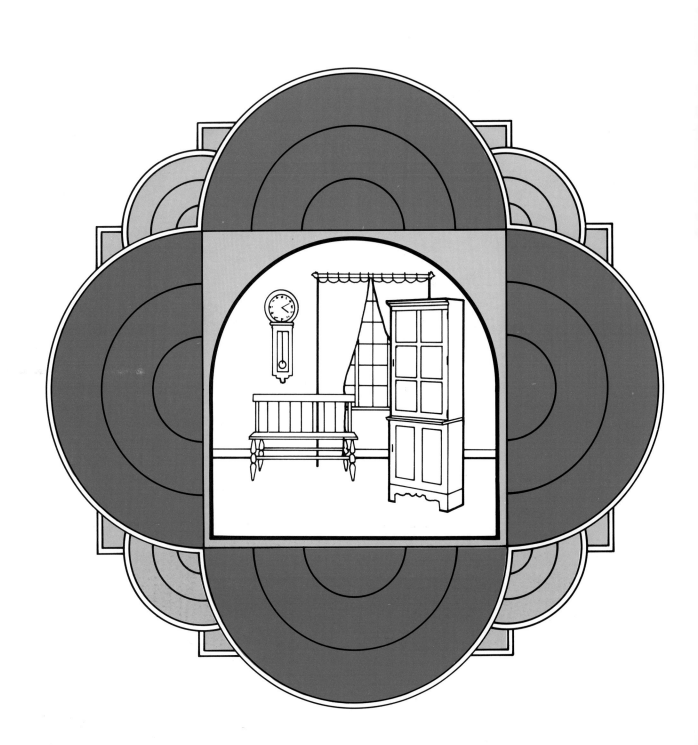

Furnishing your first home, whether it is a one-room apartment, a mobile home, or a conventional-type house, should be one of the happiest experiences of your life. Until now, the problems of home furnishings have probably not concerned you. As you grew up, you most likely took for granted the comforts of your physical environment. But now that you have a home of your own, furnishings may have suddenly taken on a new significance.

Shopping for furniture is not like shopping for clothing. If you buy the wrong dress or suit it may be hidden in the closet, but how do you hide a sofa or a floor of carpeting? These things may be part of your environment for many years, and they must please and serve your needs as well as the needs of other members of your family who will live with them now and later on. A little judicious planning now will save embarrassment later.

Purchase With a Plan

Probably the most common mistake of young people when they are furnishing their first home is that they buy too much too fast. As a result, they have a room full of cheap furniture that they are not completely happy with and that will soon need to be replaced. Remember that decorating is a continuing process, and homes with character develop slowly. Select one thing at a time and enjoy it before buying the next item. To become a discriminating customer takes time and effort, but it will pay big dividends. Your first furniture purchase should be made only after much careful study and planning. A married couple should reach some agreement as to taste, general style preferences, and price. When you begin to shop, take your time; do not be rushed into making a decision before you are satisfied. Couples should shop together because household expendi-

147

tures are usually big ones, and there must be complete understanding of and agreement on costs; otherwise, future payments may cause trouble.

Seldom do young people decorate their first apartment with a specific style of furniture in mind, and this is not important. What *is* important is that the first purchase be made with a "plan," a general theme which you wish eventually to achieve. Look for simple but well-designed pieces that can be blended into a more definite scheme later on. Avoid buying a roomful of advertised "economy" furniture. At best it will be mediocre and likely will be dated in a few years. Instead, start with one good piece of wood furniture; then fill in with an assortment of temporary items, candidly retrieved from a variety of sources. Your good piece can be a focal point and can establish a mood that will be a guide to your later purchases.

Important Things to Look for in Wood Furniture

When you are selecting furniture, you should keep three points in mind: good design, flexibility, and sturdy construction.

Design is a personal thing and should be chosen on the basis of individual taste developed through an understanding of the principles of design, with suitability and comfort in mind. Look for simple, unadorned furniture. It will serve you now and will mix with other

pieces later on. A simple classic design does not suffer from mass production; but avoid purchasing a cheap imitation of more costly, hand-carved items. Do not be misled by a current *fad*. If a piece of furniture is not right for your needs and does not appeal to you, no matter how "in" it may be at the moment, do not be pressured into buying it. And remember that you do not have to pay a lot for good design. It is quite possible to get well-designed furniture for a modest price if you shop carefully and are willing to forego unnecessary and often objectional embellishment. Put your money into *quality* and *good but simple design*.

Flexibility is an important consideration. If a piece of furniture can serve a variety of purposes, it will be useful for many years.

Construction quality must often be left to the integrity of the manufacturer and the word of the salesperson, but with wood furniture that has an exposed frame, such as a chair, it is possible to examine some points of contruction. See if it is hard or soft wood (1). Hard wood will cost more, but is well worth the difference in furniture that you will use for a long time. See if the back legs are a continuation of the frame; this makes for a stronger, more durable piece. Joints should be double doweled (2) with corner blocks fitted, glued, and screwed into place (3). If you cannot see these features, you may be able to feel them through the covering under the chair seat. Look for dovetail joints on drawers (4).

Natural woods are preferred by all age groups today. The use of oak is on the increase and has a great appeal for

HARD WOOD

①

SOFT WOOD

①

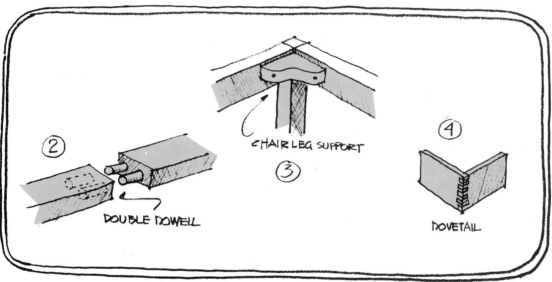

②

DOUBLE DOWELL

CHAIR LEG SUPPORT

③

④

DOVETAIL

several reasons: It takes naturally to casual life styles; it is versatile and in good supply, and it is available in a wide price range from budget groups to top-of-the-line. Look for oak in sturdy, easy-to-live-with furniture.

Colored finishes on wood furnishings are gaining in popularity; so get out your paints and brushes and liberate some of the old pieces from the attic. You will have fun and can add interest to your rooms. It is estimated that within the next ten years 50 percent of all case goods sold will be colored.

To be an intelligent shopper, you should become familiar with the style names of the most commonly used pieces of furniture. Certain identifying names have been given to different styles of furniture; and although details such as legs, arms, and backs will vary widely, the general shapes can be easily recognized.

Upholstered chairs and sofas are identified by their general shape, height from the floor, types of backs, arms, and legs. Although some details such as cushion treatment and trim will vary with the individual designer, they can usually be identified.

Many different kinds of tables are used today. Decorative details such as legs, feet, and points of design will vary according to the style of the period, but the general characteristics remain the same and can be recognized.

Case furniture is a general term for pieces of furniture used for holding things. In cabinet work it refers to the shell of a piece of furniture, such as a

(Upper left). The pedestal oak table will always be in good taste. Put it anywhere. *Courtesy of Ethan Allen.* (Above). The true elegance of simplicity is evident in this grouping of chairs and table. The stark lines of the furniture are relieved by the oriental rug and plants. *Courtesy of Thayer Coggin Inc.* (Below). The classic rush-bottom ladder-back chair is ageless. Use it in any room with traditional or modern. *Courtesy of Ethan Allen.*

151

chest of drawers, or any type of cabinet. As with chairs and tables, the details in case pieces will differ depending upon the period design, but the major characteristics remain the same. For a number of the most common styles of chairs, sofas, tables, and case pieces, see the illustrations on pages 164 and 165.

Use of Plastic in Furniture. Many furniture firms use plastic where they once used wood. See-through acrylic furniture is attractive and seems to occupy no space, but it scratches easily. Many molded plastic chairs and tables are of excellent design, are practical and durable, and come in a wide price range. The famous pedestal chair of Ero Sarrinen has become a modern classic and will always be good. It has been much copied and goes everywhere (5).

For some purposes, such as for table tops that get hard usage, plastic may serve the purpose better and will be more durable than wood. Vinyl veneer (vinyl is the term most often used for plastic surfaces; veneer is a thin layer of wood or plastic glued to the surface of a thicker backing) has the look and feel of wood; it needs no wax, stain, or varnish; it resists scratches and most household liquids; and it is easy to maintain. The veneer may be a vinyl laminate that actually contains a thin veneer of wood, or it may be either a vinyl that simulates wood graining through a photographic process or a veneer that is a combination of both.

Plastic is used also on the face of

Line and form are combined to
create two tables of simplicity and
great beauty. The juxtaposition of
circles and rectangles creates an
image most pleasing to the eye. A
touch of pattern in the bowls and
in the flowers relieves the otherwise
severe lines. These tables could
be used in any decor. *Courtesy
of Thayer Coggin Inc.*

153

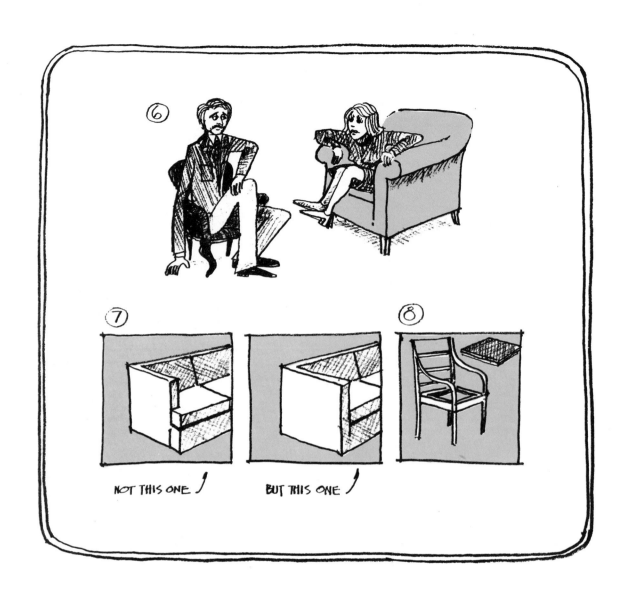

154

furniture pieces where intricate carving is often simulated. While plastic on flat surfaces can be a practical and wise choice, plastic simulated hand-carved pieces should be avoided, since they smack of pretense. Manufacturers and salesmen do not refer to these pieces as plastics but as vinyl veneers, high-pressure laminates, or molded components.

Be familiar with man-made materials in furniture, and if they are used where they serve a definite function for you, they may be a better choice than wood.

Shopping Tips for Buying Upholstered Furniture

When you shop for upholstered furniture, the first thing that catches your eye is the fabric; so consider it first. Ask about durability of the fiber, surface finish, and ease of care. Then inquire about hidden assets. What kind of cushioning does the chair or sofa have? Is it soft, comfortable, and resilient? Will it retain its shape? Can it be cleaned? Is it odorless and non-allergenic? Is it light enough to make the furniture easily movable? Comfort is of great importance in upholstered furniture. Sit in it. Check the depth of the seat and the height of the back and arms. In choosing a lounge chair for a particular person, have that person "try it on." A chair that is comfortable for one person may be uncomfortable for another (6).

Buy a chair with loose cushions on the back and seat. They can be turned and used on both sides, thus doubling the life of the fabric.

Buy a sofa with square seat cushions instead of T-shaped ones; the middle and end ones may be exchanged to increase the wear (7).

Buy dining room chairs with slip seats that are easily removed and recovered. They take less material and wear longer, and recovering is a simple matter (8).

Choose quilted, lightweight upholstery fabric rather than plain. It will wear longer.

Furniture Marketing Methods

Some understanding of furniture marketing methods will be helpful in making a purchase. For example, most furniture is presented to the customer in suites, groups, and collections.

A *suite* of furniture consists of pieces of furniture designed to be used together in a specific room. All pieces look alike and are priced as a unit, and as a rule they cannot be broken up. Two such units are a dining room suite consisting of a table, chairs, and a buffet; and a bedroom suite of a bed, chest, and dresser.

A *furniture group* is a large ensemble or collection correlated by the same design. A group may include suites for bedrooms, dining rooms, and living rooms with many extra pieces. The advantage in purchasing from a group is that pieces are coordinated, and additional items are available at any time to complete your starter-set. There is danger here, however, of a look-alike feeling that may become monotonous. Avoid doing rooms in

155

which everything matches. You can find plenty of such rooms set up in furniture stores. They lack interest and personality.

A *collection* has the look of individuality and is usually in the higher-priced market. The impression is one of a mixture of pieces thoughtfully collected over a period of time. Designs are not the same, but all will have a feeling of compatibility.

Because there are so many hidden values in furniture construction, it is important that you buy from a reputable dealer and whenever possible choose brand names that you have seen advertised nationally. Most manufacturers now supply information tags and literature with their furniture. Read all such tags carefully and check the guarantees.

What About Style?

In selecting furniture for your first home, do not be too concerned with style names. It is usually wise for young people to avoid the selection of a definite style. Their tastes frequently change after a few years, and replacement of furniture is a major expenditure. Always available is well-designed, nonperiod furniture that adapts to any style. Only the correct use of fabric in the room is necessary to create a definite mood. However, a knowledge of the different furniture styles can be helpful in providing guidelines in recognizing furniture with lasting design. The fact that some styles have stood the test of time is proof of their good design.

Find out what features distinguish one style from another, what mood is created by each, and which styles can and which cannot be compatibly used together. Use the library. Read a variety of good magazines. Examine model rooms in stores. Pay particular attention to homes you like. These will enable you to shop with more discrimination and will help you get the best value for your money.

"Fun" Furniture for Young Moderns

The present trend toward cushy upholstered modern furniture with an emphasis on the leather look, along with natural woods and chrome, has a strong appeal to young people and is being produced in prices that are within their range. Another important trend for today's young moderns is ready-made furniture that comes from the factory prefinished and ready to be easily and quickly assembled. It is either curvy or clean-cut, flexible or rigid. It is lightweight and can be easily moved and stored in very little space. It is "fun" furniture that serves many purposes and can solve many of the problems of young people on the move as well as those living in limited space.

These ready-mades are available in a number of different items. For example, three prefinished boards come in a flat cardboard box, two sections for a base and one for a top. Presto! You have a table. Add others and make bookshelves, a divider, or a bench. These come in teak or lacquered vinyl (9).

Flat-packed decorator cubes come in a wide variety of colors of vinyl wood-grain finish. Groove them together,

and you have a coffee table or an end table. Stack and interlock them to form a storage wall or a free-standing room divider. Top a single cube with a cushion for extra seating. Turn a number of them into a bench against a wall. Add foam rubber covered squares, and you will have seating for several or a bed for an overnight guest (10).

Redwood boxes come 24″ × 24″ × 9″ with holes and pegs for easy assemblage. They come ready for use, open or with dividers or drawers to fill almost any need. Make library shelves, wall storage, or a catchall.

Three contoured pieces of polyfoam covered with polyfoam become a chair when the ends fold over; unfold them, and you have a chaise (11).

Bunching pieces come designed to fit snugly together or group around a table. They can be lifted with one hand.

Stackable furniture comes in a wide array of colors and styles. Modular units stack to make a table and chairs for indoor or outdoor use, then disassemble for easy moving and compact storing (12).

Bunk beds are available for quick and easy assemblage by means of a skillfully made slotting system. The frames at the ends will serve as ladders.

Fashions in furniture come and go, and it is good to keep abreast of new trends. Some useful and versatile "fun" pieces can be very helpful to "fill in" as you carefully create the home you envision for your future. But when you look for a substantial piece of wood furniture to fit into your overall plan, do not be in a hurry to buy. If your first purchase is well designed, with simple uncluttered lines, it will give a lifetime of satisfaction and pleasure.

A Survey Report of Furniture Purchases

In a survey of 983 in-home interviews conducted in the fall of 1973 for the Newspaper Advertising Bureau to determine buying habits of young people, they found that the average homemaker requires 3.4 shopping trips to make a furniture purchase, and six out of ten are won over by price or a special sale. More than half of the eighteen- to twenty-nine-year-olds surveyed purchased their furniture from a furniture specialty store, 10 percent from a national chain, 10 percent from a discount department store, and 8 percent from a department store.

Those who shopped most carefully, the survey showed, were better educated and from higher income families. College-educated women, for example, typically made 3.8 shopping trips compared with 2.8 shopping trips for those with high school educations or less. Only 20 percent mentioned style or looks as reasons for buying. Quality was mentioned by 13 percent and store reputation by 9 percent. Indicating they would buy the same way again, 71 percent appeared satisfied with a recent purchase. However, 29 percent indicated they would buy differently. Of those who said they would buy differently, 40 percent said they would choose better quality and 38 percent said they would shop around more. (*Home Furnishings Daily*, June 3, 1974.)

The above survey seems to bear out

(Upper left). A deluxe round dining-game set for today's way of living. Made of thermoplastic, the lines are clean and simple. Use it anywhere. *Courtesy of Syroco.* (Lower far left). A distinctive grouping for casual, durable indoor-outdoor furniture, made of tough thermoplastic. *Courtesy of Syroco.* (Above). A sleek wall piece can be storage for a myriad of things. *Courtesy of Thayer Coggin Inc.* (Below). This handsome, sturdy table of large scale and natural oak veneer will serve many purposes. *Courtesy of Lane.*

161

(Right). A serving cart is a useful as well as a decorative item of furniture. Care will increase the beauty. *Courtesy of Ethan Allen.* (Below). The small-scaled drop-leaf table is particularly appropriate when space is limited. This classic piece will always be in style. *Courtesy of Ethan Allen.*

162

the need for the consumer to be better informed and to shop more carefully.

Furniture Care

Elementary as it sounds, regular dusting and polishing are the best guardians of the beauty of a fine furniture finish. Grandma with her feather-duster understood the secret of preventing the accumulation of surface soil, often abrasive and harmful to a carefully rubbed finish. Today you have a choice of excellent waxes and polishes which, if used regularly, deepen the luster and clarity of fine finishes as they maintain an important protective film. Accidents will occur, and for the care and treatment of these we present the suggestions below. First aid for minor scratches, blemishes, burns, and stains might include some items from the following furniture first aid chart.

Furniture First Aid

For minor scratches. Use a wax stick in a matching color to fill the scratch. These are inexpensive and usually available at paint, hardware, or furniture stores. Rub in well. Wipe with a soft, dry cloth and apply your preferred polish.

White spots — cause unknown. Rub blemish with cigar or cigarette ashes, using cloth dipped in wax, lubricating oil, vegetable shortening, lard, or salad oil. Wipe off immediately and rewax with your preferred polish.

Alcohol spots. Method A: Rub with finger dipped in paste wax, silver polish, linseed oil, or moistened cigar ash. Rewax with your preferred polish. Method B: On some finishes a quick application of ammonia will do the trick. Put a few drops on a damp cloth and rub the spot. Follow immediately with polish.

Water marks. Marks or rings from wet glasses are common on tables, especially if these surfaces have not been waxed. Wax cannot prevent damage when liquids are allowed to stand on the finish indefinitely. However, it will keep them from being absorbed immediately, thus giving you time to wipe liquid before it damages the finish. If water marks appear, here are some tips to try: Method A: Apply preferred wax or polish with fine 3/0 steel wool, rubbing lightly. Method B: Place a clean, thick blotter over the ring and press with a warm (not hot) iron. Repeat until ring disappears.

Candle wax. Hold an ice cube on the wax for a few seconds to harden it, but wipe up melted ice immediately. Crumble off as much wax as can be removed with the fingers and then scrape gently with a dull knife. Rub briskly with a clean cloth saturated with liquid wax, wiping dry with a clean cloth. Repeat until mark disappears.

Milk spots. When milk — or foods containing milk or cream — are allowed to remain on furniture, the effect of the lactic acid is like that of a mild paint or varnish remover. Wipe up the spilled food as quickly as possible. If the spots show, clean with wax. Then follow the tips under *alcohol spots.* (Courtesy Ethan Allen.)

163

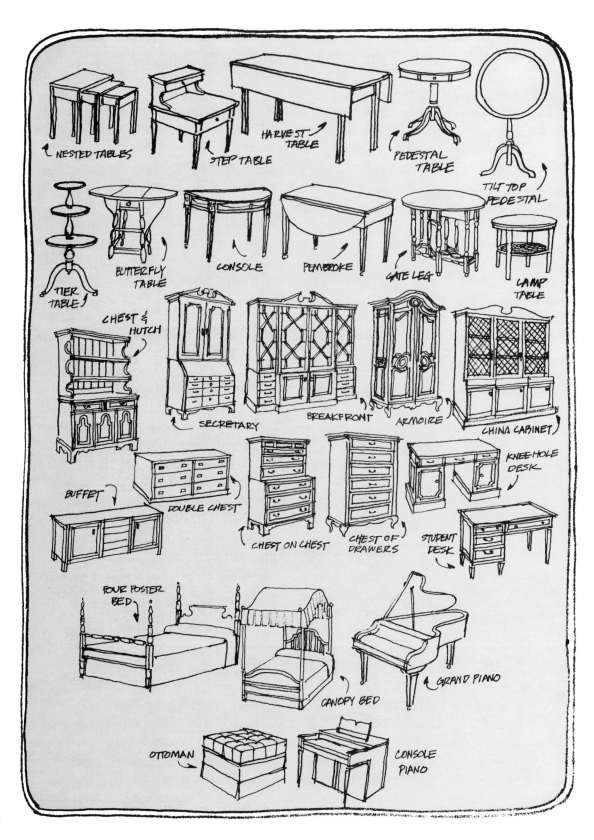

NESTED TABLES

STEP TABLE

HARVEST TABLE

PEDESTAL TABLE

TILT TOP PEDESTAL

TIER TABLE

BUTTERFLY TABLE

CONSOLE

PEMBROKE

GATE LEG

LAMP TABLE

CHEST & HUTCH

SECRETARY

BREAKFRONT

ARMOIRE

CHINA CABINET

BUFFET

DOUBLE CHEST

CHEST ON CHEST

CHEST OF DRAWERS

KNEE-HOLE DESK

STUDENT DESK

FOUR POSTER BED

CANOPY BED

GRAND PIANO

OTTOMAN

CONSOLE PIANO

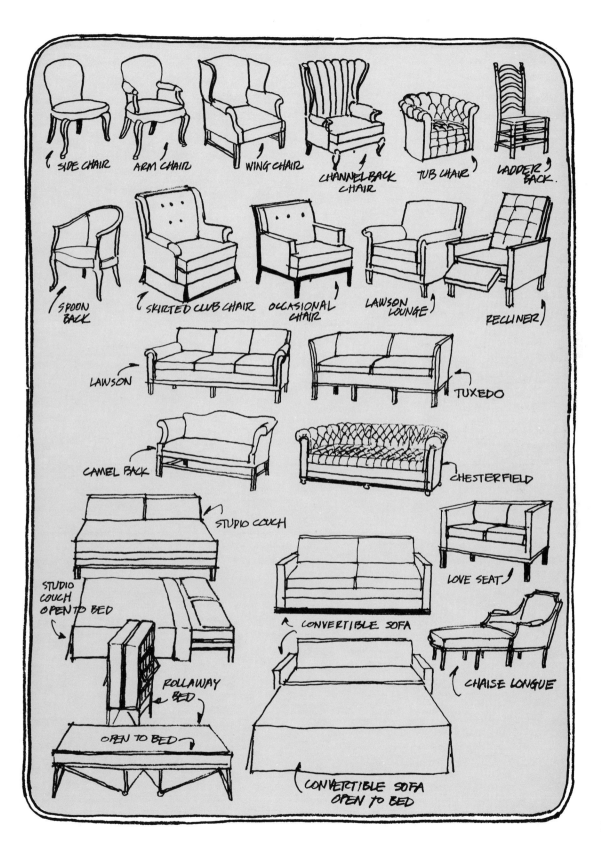

SIDE CHAIR

ARM CHAIR

WING CHAIR

CHANNEL BACK CHAIR

TUB CHAIR

LADDER BACK

SPOON BACK

SKIRTED CLUB CHAIR

OCCASIONAL CHAIR

LAWSON LOUNGE

RECLINER

LAWSON

TUXEDO

CAMEL BACK

CHESTERFIELD

STUDIO COUCH

STUDIO COUCH OPEN TO BED

ROLLAWAY BED

OPEN TO BED

CONVERTIBLE SOFA

CONVERTIBLE SOFA OPEN TO BED

LOVE SEAT

CHAISE LONGUE

Suggestions and Assignments for Part 7: Fun With Furniture

Suggested Teaching Aids and Procedures

1. Show illustrations of both good and bad design.
2. Show illustrations of dual-purpose furniture and encourage discussion and ideas from the class.
3. If there is a technical school in your area, invite someone to come in and illustrate with simple pieces of furniture the things to look for in well-constructed furniture.
4. Suggest that students examine furniture they have at home to determine quality of construction.
5. Assign students to look through local newspapers and current magazines and clip examples of well-designed and poorly designed furniture.
6. Have students become familiar with the common names of furniture styles in sofas, chairs, tables, and case pieces.

Student Assignments

Left to the discretion of the teacher.

COLORPLATE 24. This do-it-yourself room was made from natural wood with a minimum of skill. Pieces of unusual fabric in a variety of patterns but with the same color scheme were used for the cushions. All is set off by the rich red rug. *Courtesy of Evans Products Company.*

Stretching Your Dollar

COLORPLATE 25. Eclectic is the
word for this appealing attic room.
The sleek molded furniture is
emphasized against the painted
floor and the Bokhara rug. These,
with the antique chest of drawers,
the tiffany chandelier, and the
greenery, all add up to a fun room
with a variety of uses. *Courtesy
of Chromcraft.*

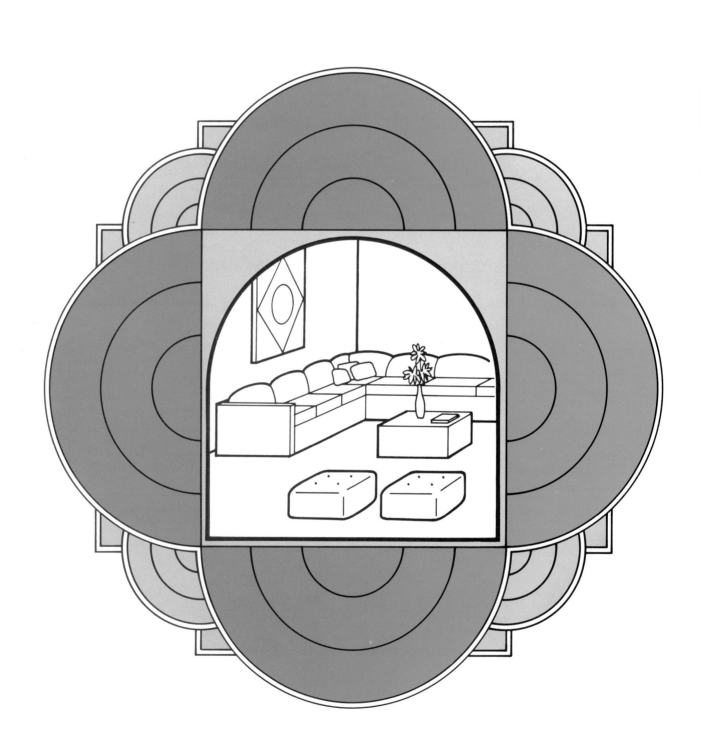

Budget buying does not mean buying only inexpensive items; it means getting the most value for the money you have to spend. Getting your money's worth involves knowing value and recognizing that a bargain is not what you *pay* but what you *get* for what you pay. Be honest when you shop. Do not pretend to the salesman that you can afford to spend more than you can. Decide in advance and frankly state what you can pay. Then search until you find good design that fits your needs. It can be done.

Whether you are starting to furnish your first apartment or are redoing what you already have, remember that it is the idea and not the dollar that is important. Use your imagination. Plan to do as much of the work as possible yourself. Many do-it-yourself kits assist you with numerous projects. Besides saving money, you will find real pleasure and satisfaction.

Multipurpose Furniture

The young homemaker who likes efficiency and organization and thus keeps an uncluttered house can find good buys in basic, hard-working dual or multipurpose furniture. For example, a sectional table can serve as an individual snack bar, or its sections can be combined for group dining. Its easily movable seats can serve as extra seating, or they can be tucked away. Shelves are handy for storage when part of the table becomes a desk, and when it is divided in half, it makes a pair of consoles (1).

A drop-front cabinet is another piece of multipurpose furniture. It takes little space; it provides storage; and it becomes a desk, a dining table, a cutting table, or a surface for numerous uses (2). Or a table top with two sets of screw-on legs may serve as a coffee table, a dining table, or a desk (3). Also, a redwood

171

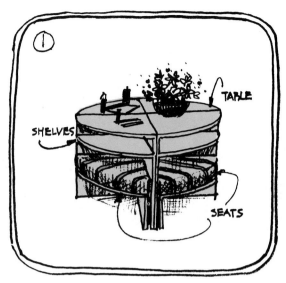

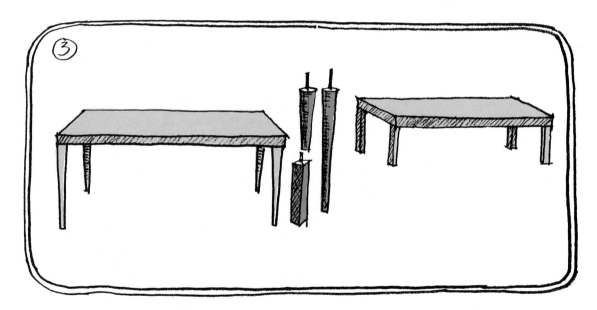

picnic table with benches may be purchased in the off season for very little cost and used in your dinette with padded cushions to give a feeling of comfort and permanency. Later, the set may go onto the patio. Folding camp stools with gay cushions can serve as extra seating in any room; basket stools with padded tops can double for family room seating and storage; and wicker baskets can serve as attractive coffee tables or end tables. Watch for other well-designed multi-purpose furniture. It is not a new idea, but you may be surprised at what you find.

Bargains in Furniture

Read your local papers for floor model furniture sales. These pieces may have a few scratches on them, but these

would appear in your home in a few months, anyway. Check your local area for a railroad-damaged goods outlet. You can often find furniture and appliances with slight damage selling at great discounts. These damages can usually be repaired with little cost or skill. Also watch your local newspaper for railroad auctions of unclaimed furniture. The bargains you can sometimes find there will astound you. It is usually possible to preview these items in advance, to help you bid intelligently.

Do-it-yourself Furniture

Don't overlook the many possibilities of making your own furniture. Wherever you live, locate the nearest lumberyard. They usually have a pile of rejects and scrap lumber that you

173

may have for carrying them away. Make frequent trips to watch for usable pieces. Odd lengths and scrap pieces of lumber obtained at little or no cost can, with a little imagination and skill, be made into useful and necessary household items. If you can make a box, you have all the skill you need. Scrap pieces of wood, supplemented by additional lumber, can also produce furniture items at surprisingly low cost and with pleasing results. The well-known Parsons table, for example, is a must for a room with a modern look and is easy to make (4). A sturdy, easily constructed boxlike base, when fitted with a single mattress and back cushions, can become a sofa by day and a bed by night and can provide valuable storage space as well (5). Or build a simple wall-hung storage unit for books, stereo and TV. It can be done very inexpensively, and you can take it with you when you go.

Stock items in lumber yards offer many possibilities for building inexpensive pieces of household furniture. Small, milled items of wood can be

added to homemade or plain, un-
painted furniture to give it a custom
look. Classic moldings and shelf
edging can make a simple piece look
like a much more expensive one.
When moldings are glued to drawers,
to sides of case furniture, or to a plain
door, they give the effect of carving;
and when applied to the lower part of
a wall, with another molding added
above, they can produce the illusion of
a wood-paneled dado (6). Wood
balusters (supports for a rail or legs of
a table) — old or new — have many

uses. Large ones mounted on wooden blocks with a screw or a nail on the top become attractive candle holders (7). Rows of balusters glued to a base make a handsome divider. Twelve- to fourteen-inch squares of wood made into cubes and topped by a custom door or plywood slab make a long coffee table. The cubes can be useful in children's rooms later on. One half-circle of plywood with a laminated plastic top supported on a pedestal of angled wood strips makes an excellent table for a small area.

Keep your eyes open for discarded crating lumber, too. It can be put to many uses. Stained or sprayed, it takes on the appearance of barn wood that is so popular. And don't overlook the possibilities of orange crates. Painted or lined and edged with wallpaper or fabric, they can be stacked to provide colorful storage for stereo records or for a variety of other things.

Watch also for discarded packing barrels. You need only fasten a round piece of plywood on the top and cover it with fabric, and you have a table for many purposes. And the barrel will store things (8). Be on the lookout, too, for wooden spools abandoned by utility companies. These come in many sizes and make sturdy tables. Check your supermarkets and hardware stores for vegetable crates and other sturdy packing boxes.

Make a Parsons table out of a cardboard box: leave one of the long sides intact for the table top; remove the opposite side; cut out the four remaining sides, leaving 2 to 2 1/2 inches at the top and at the ends; cover with three coats of enamel paint, sanding after each application; when the third coat is thoroughly dry and sanded, apply a coat of high gloss shellac. The result will be a handsome coffee table of surprising sturdiness. Smaller ones make convenient end tables. Or make a number to be stacked and brought out for company snacks (9).

Make cubes out of scrap lumber and cover them with carpet scraps or squares purchased on special sale. Hinge one side to provide storage. Your friends will love sitting on them.

Treasures Out of Discards

The satisfaction of making something useful, even beautiful, out of what someone else has discarded not only saves money but satisfies a creative urge. The number of worthwhile items that can be salvaged by someone with a trained eye is unlimited. Sometimes discarded furniture, because of poor design, must be restyled to serve a modern need; but with a little imagination this restyling can be a profitable and rewarding undertaking. Second-hand and goodwill stores abound in such items. And never pass up a pile of "junk" without a scrutinizing look.

Look for the city dump. If you have never encountered a dump digger, you have missed an experience. After a few visits to the dump, you may become one yourself. Pickups won't always be lucrative, but you will sometimes be amazed at what people discard. Often an unusual item — and occasionally

176

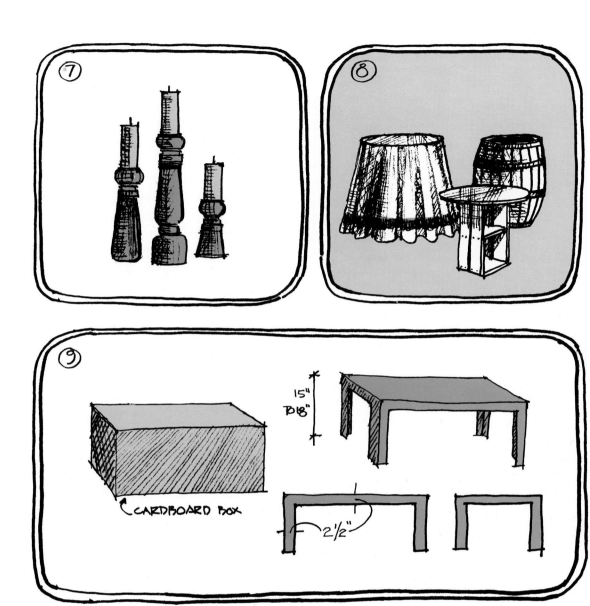

7

8

9

CARDBOARD BOX

15"
TO 18"

2½"

177

a rare one — will show up. Dumps aren't easy to get to, but check the schedule of deliveries. There are ways of getting to these piles of peoples' rejects. Give it a try. You might have fun and might find something you can salvage, besides.

And don't overlook car cemeteries. A single car seat mounted on a plywood base becomes a comfortable chair, and a full seat makes a sturdy love seat (10). Metal rims from wheels fastened together with epoxy glue, painted, and cushioned will double as a low table and as extra seating.

Large pieces of furniture can often be taken apart and used for a variety of purposes. Old radio cabinets, for example, have many possibilities. Try placing an old-fashioned china cabinet on top of one. Line the china cabinet with velvet, install interior lighting, add new hardware to both, and you may have a focal point of great charm — even of value. An old filing cabinet may be cut into two parts, topped with an old door, and turned into a kneehole desk. A long, outdated treadle sewing machine base with a plywood top laminated with vinyl or wood veneer becomes a handsome buffet with a Mediterranean look (11). Brass beds need only to be polished and backed with colored felt or velvet, and a fashionable headboard results. All manner of old beds can be restyled, cut down, painted, and padded.

Old dressers that are too deep for today's limited space can be cut vertically and put side by side to form shelves (12). A dresser becomes a chest of drawers when the mirror is

179

removed and hung to expand space elsewhere, and an ancient buffet can also become a chest when the legs are removed. A sturdy round oak table, lowered, becomes a coffee table or, cut in half, makes a pair of side tables. Revitalizing an old trunk or footlocker with paint is often done; but try using patchwork. Glue an underlayer of a fabric such as felt to give a soft backing, then apply colorful patchwork inside and out. Everyone will admire it.

One with a perceptive eye will see numerous possibilities in many small discarded articles. For example, old iron gates make handsome headboards; for decorative purposes, a metal register from an obsolete hot-air furnace can be the top for a lamp or a coffee table; ornately carved table legs may form the base for a new, handsome, glass-top table; an odd piece of wood carving may appear as a decorative wall shelf or bracket; an old picture frame supported by a luggage rack will make a coffee table (13); discarded window frames placed against a windowless wall, filled with plants, and lighted from behind will create the illusion of a garden room. Old wood shutters have a myriad of uses: they can conceal unsightly radiators, serve as room dividers, make a backdrop for a seating arrangement, and substitute for drapery — to mention only a few.

If a piece of furniture is of good design, good wood, and sound construction, it is worth refinishing. Many a prized antique has been rescued after being hidden for years under numerous layers of paint. To successfully bring old furniture back to life does not require any special talent. What it does require is a desire, a great deal of patience, and a lot of hard work, plus careful preparation with all the necessary materials of good quality close at hand. But the satisfaction of restoring a good piece to its original beauty is worth the effort. Learn to upholster. This, too, is hard work, but it pays big dividends.

Refinishing Furniture

(The following instructions for refinishing furniture [through "Finishing fundamentals"] are reprinted by permission of *Home Planning and Design* magazine #59.)

Wood finishing requires a modest amount of talent, quality materials, and a great deal of patience and preparation. Here are some tips on how to get the most out of your future wood finishing projects.

The success of any wood finishing project depends on (1) a clean surface, which is free of dirt, dust, wax, oil, stains, smudges, and grease; and (2) a smooth surface, free of dents, gouges, and scratches.

Preparing old surfaces

For any interior wood surface where a previous clear finish is dull or worn but not cracked or peeling to bare wood, simply wash the surface with a solvent to remove accumulated wax, dirt and grease. A solution of TSP (trisodium phosphate, available at any paint store) is a good solvent for this purpose. Rinse thoroughly and wipe dry with clean cloths while the surface is still wet. Sand lightly with fine paper until smooth and remove all dust with a tack rag or a vacuum.

Complete refinishing

If the previous finish is badly deteriorated, chipped, crazed, or peeling, remove the old finish entirely with a *quality* paint and varnish remover. Don't be fooled here by bargain prices — buying inexpensive, poor quality remover is really poor economy. Even with top-brand removers, several coats may be required; so flow on the liquid generously and allow it to set for a reasonable length of time. When the finish is easily lifted, remove with steel wool, rags, or putty knife. Always work with the grain to avoid scratching. Allow to dry thoroughly, then remove all dust and loose foreign matter by brushing or wiping with a lint-free cloth. If the wood is smooth after the use of remover, no sanding is required.

Preparing new surfaces

For wood surfaces not previously finished, use fine sandpaper to remove minor smudges and soil marks. To remove severe stains, use a bleach or "prep" agent, applied according to the manufacturer's instructions.

Filling

Some unfinished woods require filling before finishing. The basic purpose of a paste filler is to fill open grain of coarse-textured woods such as oak, mahogany, or walnut so that the final finish will be level and smooth. Filling also prevents excessive penetration of stains or finishing coats and allows greater, more economical coverage. On most open-grained woods, the paste filler should precede staining.

Staining techniques

After the surface has been properly sanded and dusted with a tack cloth, apply the stain by rag, sponge, roller, or brush. Be sure to work only a small area at a time. While the stain is still wet, wipe off excess stain with the grain, using a dampened, soft, absorbent material (a cloth or sponge). Stains can be light and delicate or deep in mood. The longer a stain is allowed to stand before being wiped with the damp cloth, the deeper the color. So remove excess stain until you obtain the color depth and grain appeal you seek. Stains may also be lightened before application by diluting with the proper solvent (as recommended only by the manufacturer on the label).

For large area staining (paneling) use a medium nap paint roller. Stain one section at a time (from top to bottom), and wipe off excess stain before it sets. A helper speeds the job — one applying the stain, the other wiping.

Staining softwoods

Each wood takes stain differently. The softwoods, such as pine and other conifers, are more absorbent and accept

182

stain more readily. Test a small section of wood before you begin. With some softwoods, a sealer may be necessary to assure uniformity of the stain.

Finishing fundamentals

1) Be sure the working surface *and* the working area are as dust-free as possible.
2) Use a clean brush and container. Small bits of dust and debris can spoil an otherwise perfect job.
3) Apply finish in thin coats, brushing out well to avoid runs and sags.
4) Work in long strokes from end to end of the surface to avoid lap marks, in the same direction of the grain if possible.
5) If bubbles linger, brush again lightly but never re-work more than necessary.
6) Hand-sand lightly between coats with fine paper and dust with a tack rag.

(Above). A do-it-yourself room with paneled walls. Touches of the Gay Nineties in a family heirloom chair and old rescued windows have real character. *Courtesy of Armstrong Cork Company.* (Below). Carefree living with laminates. The graceful curves of the chairs are a pleasing contrast to the sharp corners of the parsons table. *Courtesy of Thayer Coggin Inc.*

You'll find that the final finishing is actually the easiest part of the entire process — patient and thorough preparation before you begin is the key to any fine finish.

The pieces of furniture to be found and the purposes they can serve are endless; and the satisfaction of turning an eyesore into a useful or decorative object is a real incentive to keep searching. Availability of lucrative sources will vary in different areas, but some can be found in most localities. Used furniture stores and goodwill stores of various kinds are almost everywhere. Watch for new acquisitions by making regular visits; articles of best value do not often remain long. Do not overlook items that have been languishing, sometimes for years, in basements and dark corners. This is where an occasional treasure is found. Check your local newspaper for items offered at real "sacrifice prices." Rummage through family attics and garage sales. Attend auctions, and be on hand when old buildings in your area are being torn down. As a novice, you will undoubtedly bring home a lot of junk to begin with, but after much study and perseverance, you will be delighted with the rewards of "junking."

New Surfaces for Old with Paint

Painting is the quickest and least expensive way of bringing new life to worn surfaces. Whether it be the exterior of a house, a nondescript door, interior walls, an ugly fireplace, or a battered piece of furniture, the right coat of paint will work real magic. Although colors must always be chosen with great care, the power of color in making the first-last-and-always impression must never be overlooked. New paints and effective methods of application should dispel any fears a novice may have about the outcome of a do-it-yourself job. Today's paints are easy to apply; they dry with incredible speed, and they hold up under hard wear and numerous washings.

Besides the standard paintbrush, there are now tools to speed up painting and produce a smooth, professional surface. A roller will do an excellent job in large areas, such as walls and ceilings, and in a fraction of the time that it takes to paint the same area with a brush. For small areas and for furniture, however, a brush is still the most efficient tool. For hard-to-get-at chinks in radiators, shutters, grills, wickerwork, and metal surfaces, spray-can painting is neat and quick. Be sure to protect everything not to be sprayed.

Some new paints on the market today have remarkable properties: they can cover any surface; they hold up under the most trying use, and they produce surfaces never before obtainable. But it is important that you choose the right paint for the surface to be covered. Following are the most used paints on the market today.

Linseed-oil paints still account for 40 percent of the paints sold today, but each year the percentage is declining. They are still used for plaster and plasterboard, woodwork, metal, and wood siding.

Plastics have invaded the paint can. Plastic resins stirred into newer solutions are the base for a range of paints which produce extremely durable surfaces. They are odorless, quick-drying, washable, and easily applied. Some resemble baked-on enamel and are almost as impervious, and an exterior paint is practically blister free.

Latex paints are water-mix paints so that the clean-up job is made easy. Just wash rollers, brushes, and

COLORPLATE 26. A room to which any boy would like to take a friend to spend the night. It is about the closest thing to being out in the open. *Courtesy of Armstrong Cork Company.*

185

COLORPLATE 27. A basement room needn't be drab. Use some cheerful colors and a lot of imagination. *Courtesy of Armstrong Cork Company.*

186

drippings with water. Latex leaves no overlap marks; it is quick-drying, and its characteristic odor fades quickly. The difference between indoor and outdoor latex is that outdoor latex "breathes"; thus the moisture may escape, eliminating blistering. Latex paints are recommended for plaster or plasterboard, masonry, wood siding, acoustical tile, and metal. Since latex includes several varieties, one must depend on familiar and reputable brand names.

Alkyd paints are resin enamel paints which were introduced about 1960. They are very popular for the following reasons: they are faster drying; they are more resistant to yellowing; lap marks made by the brush or the roller blend into one another as the paint dries; and one coat will generally be sufficient. The alkyds are produced in high gloss, semigloss, and flat coatings. Alkyd enamels are solvent mixed and must be thinned with turpentine or solvent. They are recommended for plaster or plasterboard, woodwork, and wood siding, and are probably best for metal.

Epoxy paints are newcomers to the market, having been on the shelves only since 1962. They come in two classifications. The first is ready-mixed in a single can. The second group is a two-stage finish, or catalyzed epoxy. The latter, used as directed, puts a tilelike coating on almost any surface. After it hardens, this coating can be scratched, struck, or marked with crayon or pencil and can still be washed back to high gloss. Epoxies may be used on such surfaces as worn laundry tubs, basement walls, shower stalls, and swimming pools. They will adhere to almost any clean surface.

Important to know are the basic types of paint and what can be expected from each. Whatever paint you buy, get a quality product, and remember that good preparation of the surface is important. No matter how good the paint, it will not adhere to a dirty surface. Always read the label on the can and follow the instructions.

Fabric, Fabric Everywhere

There is no surer way of rejuvenating a room than using fabric. The market abounds with materials — for every purpose — that are durable, washable, and inexpensive. They need only to be used with artistic imagination. Ticking is good for walls, slipcovers, drapery, bedspreads, and a myriad of other uses. Add some braid or fringe to give just the right touch. Unbleached muslin, canvas, and burlap are three wonderfully versatile fabrics. There are also colorful cottons, rayons, acetates, polyesters, acrylics, and nylons in unlimited textures, patterns, and colors.

If you live in a metropolitan center, locate a mill-end store. It may be a bit out of the way, but the real values you can get there will be worth any extra effort. Watch for special sales and bargain tables. The right fabric can liven up the most nondescript rooms. Cover an old table with a floor-length skirt, make a new dust ruffle and bedspread, or pad a headboard. Cover a

battered chest of drawers with an inexpensive cotton, add oversized knobs, and you have a delightful piece of furniture (14). Cover damaged tops of desks or shelves with felt or burlap; they both come in 72-inch widths. (Don't forget to spray the fabrics with scotchguard.) If your sofa is wearing, make a lot of cushions of odd sizes and shapes from sewing scraps or remnants, add left-over fringe and tape, and bank them on the sofa. Worn areas disappear. Cover large pieces of foam rubber to make extra floor seating. Young people love them.

If you like gingham, use it lavishly in a bedroom. Cover walls and beds with it, and hang it at the window.

And sheets! The wonders you can work with sheets are endless. You can buy them in a full range of colors and in bold or delicate florals, stripes, or geometrics. You save money. A regular double bed has about seven yards of 40-inch fabric; divide its cost by seven and compare the price with comparable materials. If you watch for specials and seconds, the cost will be still less. Use sheets for drapery, table skirts, bed flounces, dressing tables; quilt them for a bedspread, or hang them from a ceiling rod to give the effect of a four-poster bed. They are durable; they wash and dry quickly; they require little or no ironing; and they are work-savers since you use the wide hem.

And towels! Watch for sales and seconds. Beautiful velvety ones come in all colors, patterns, and sizes. Use them for table cloths, table runners, place mats, and napkins. Cover foam cushions to be used on the floor or smaller cushions to be used on the sofa or bed. Make a bedspread. Hang them at your windows. Try making a mushroom hassock (15). A wall organizer can be inexpensive and colorful, and it helps to keep track of things (16).

Denim is in, plain or faded, and probably to stay. Because blue jeans

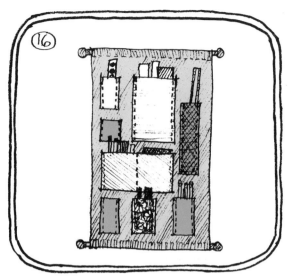 

are one of America's most durable traditions, denim for homes will likely also become part of the permanent American scene. Denim is durable and versatile. Put it on your walls; make slip covers, a head board, or a bedspread; or upholster with it. Cover a bean bag. You can use any thing that strikes your fancy for trim: vinyl, nail heads, braid, and fringe. You will have fun, and your friends will copy you.

Make a window shade out of fabric and see it glow with the light. Applique cutouts from fabric onto window shades (17). Cover strips of pine with a gay print; place them vertically at regular intervals along a dull wall; repeat the same fabric at the window, and see the room take on a lively charm. Covering a shabby chair with a new slip cover can be an effec-

tive and inexpensive way of dressing up an old piece of furniture. Make it yourself. With the new miracle stretch fabrics and nylon fastener tape, it will fit like upholstery.

If you use your imagination, you will see endless possibilities for budget decorating in dime stores. For example, have you thought of sewing together inexpensive dishcloths to make novelty weave semi-sheet curtains? Try it. When joined together, the small, inexpensive braided rugs you find there make attractive casual rugs that will go in modern or traditional rooms. Have you explored the potential of colorfully printed feed sacks? Try stuffing them to make great pillows. Stitch them together for drapery or wash them to take up the shrinkage, then press them and glue them to a wall to make a "fun" room (18).

Be always on the alert for ordinary fabrics at budget prices that can be used in unordinary ways to give

189

personality to your rooms. When you have established the habit of looking for fabric with "possibilities," you will be surprised at what you can find. And the result of your efforts will be enormously rewarding.

Accessories: The Importance of Little Things

One of the goals in decorating a room is to give it a feeling of warmth. Warmth as used here has nothing to do with temperature; it is rather a feeling of pleasure and friendliness that makes people want to linger. It is a feeling worth striving for. But how is such an atmosphere achieved? Color, for one thing, can give a room warmth, as can fabrics, carpets, and woods. But the little things, the finishing touches, are the important things that give that personal feeling of real warmth. Books, for example, give a feeling of personal interest and enjoyment. Flowers, too, show evidence that someone cares. And art and music add an intimate touch. A room containing these ingredients will be sure to have warmth and personality.

An accessory can be almost anything but should never be just something to fill up space. If an item is neither useful, beautiful, nor meaningful to you, it has no place in your home. It is much better to leave the space empty until you find something that meets at least one of these requirements. In fact, an empty space in a

(Left). Here it is — "everybody's" old basement, not really right for anything. (Below). With careful planning, minimal expense, and a few handy remedies for concealing the room's shortcomings, the basement becomes a family center for music and games. *Courtesy of Armstrong Cork Company.*

room gives one a comfortable feeling; don't fill every nook and cranny. Some accessories have a necessary function, such as clocks, lamps, mirrors, fire tools, and cushions; but these should also enhance the room and must be carefully chosen. Accessories need not be new. Fragments of old beauty can add distinctive charm and can lend character to an otherwise dull room. Objects which may have been collecting dust in attics for years may be salvaged and put to new uses.

One of the greatest challenges in beautifying your home is making attractive compositions out of little things. The secret lies in training your eye to see beauty, form, and space relationships. In arranging a number of items, you can avoid a cluttered look by using items which are in some way related, such as in shape, color, or purpose. Arrange small items on a

tray for convenience and a feeling of unity. The desire to display one's prized possessions is universal. If the items you have collected are worth acquiring, they are worth displaying. The collection does not need to be large, but whatever it consists of, devise a way of grouping the items. If you artistically display the objects you cherish, they will give you daily enjoyment; your friends will find pleasure in them, and your room will take on a personal character.

Books Are Like Friends

"A room without books is a body without a soul," said Cicero. Books can do more than anything — except people — to add life and friendliness to a home. A room never needs to feel empty of furnishings; there is always a way to provide for displaying books. Straight planks supported by decorative cement blocks or floor tiles, either painted or left natural, will make an attractive book wall. Metal strips with adjustable

brackets set to accommodate wide and narrow and long and short shelves will add an interesting irregularity to a room when books and other objects of interest are artfully displayed. Built-in shelves can serve as a room divider (19) or can be fitted into niches, odd corners, and around windows and doors to utilize unused space at very little expense (20). With so many types of flexible shelves readily available and easily installed, books can be kept anywhere. No room has a mood that would preclude them. No color scheme is so complete that it cannot be enhanced by the warm tones and textures of books. Every child needs bookshelves in his room and at a height he can reach. In any bedroom, headboards for book storage are convenient for bedtime reading. Kitchens need handy shelves for reference books. No study area is complete without bookshelves. Books, like flowers, are never out of place and, like friends, we need them always close at hand.

Flowers and Growing Plants Show You Care

Of all the accessories that make up the final touches of your home, nothing can do for a room what a bouquet of live foliage and flowers can do. Whatever the time of year, you can find something from which you can make a floral arrangement to bring delight into your home. Look around your kitchen; there are numerous possibilities for a center piece: group a variety of vegetables from your crisper and see what happens; try making a nosegay out of a bunch of radishes, or surround a head of cauliflower with some parsley. Experiment. You may surprise yourself.

There is a real joy in gathering small flowers, unknown weeds, and interesting branches and gracefully arranging them. And have some growing plants. Make a garden around a window (21). Group plants in containers of various heights, shapes, and textures. An old wicker planter

193

is at home anywhere. Spray it and fill it with plants (22). Hang a basket by a window. Fill a window ledge or tuck a tiny plant anywhere you find a spot.

If you are serious about flower arranging, you may be interested in learning the principles of the three basic styles: Oriental, traditional, and contemporary. If you prefer an un-studied bouquet, forget the rules and let your own taste be your guide. Train your eye to see beauty in the common-place things in nature and bring them indoors to give lasting pleasure. The beauty they create is absolutely free.

Take a Needle and Some Yarn

So you aren't skillful with your hands! Don't let it worry you. The things that can be done with a minimum of skill will amaze you.

Make a cobwebby tapestry. Use odds and ends of interesting threads and yarns in varying sizes and colors. On a neutral warp, weave your own design (23). Your friends will try to copy it.

Make a rug. Complete kits in a wide variety of styles and patterns are available.

Sew a canvas headboard, window shutters, or a room divider. Simply applique one fabric upon another. It takes a minimum of sewing skills, and design possibilities are unlimited. Motifs may be found in children's coloring books, in art and design guides, or on wrapping paper. Inspira-tion may come from nature and from items on your kitchen shelves. You may find a creative talent you did not know you had (24).

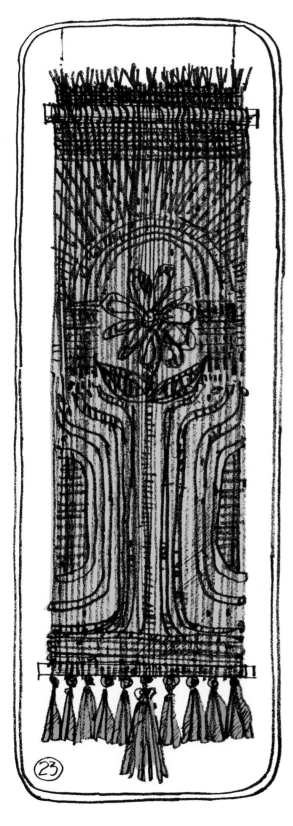

195

Learn how to do macrame. You can make window hangings that substitute for curtains and drapery, wall decorations, holders for hanging plants, and many other useful and decorative items.

More Ideas from Here and There

Create an exciting foyer. If you have no entrance hall, make one. Make a divider for privacy and interest. String colored beads, bright plastic straws, or small pine cones on fish line and attach it to a rod at the top and bottom, or use a variety of yarn. Or fashion a standing screen. The simplest do-it-yourself frame with hinges attached will serve as a foundation. Cover it with wallpaper, fabric, or needlework. Let your imagination run riot and dare to be original. The first impression people get when they enter your home is an important one. Make it something very special.

If walls need help and money is scarce, paint a super graphic. Look for ideas in design books or make your own design. In a small hallway, cover a wall with old newspapers, colorful wrapping paper, posters, or maps (the kind service stations give away). It will be a conversation piece.

If you would like interesting texture on a wall, locate some farmer's gunny sacks. They cost very little. Remove the stitching, wash them to take up shrinkage, and glue them to the wall. If you want a color, spray it.

Watch for good buys on wall board. Its cost sometimes is amazingly low, and you can install it yourself. To prevent edge splinters and chips in cutting, lay the panel face up and put masking tape along the cutting line. You can make a room look as though it were done by a professional.

Put mirrors in inexpensive picture frames of a variety of sizes and shapes. Group them together over a piece of furniture, and see how the wall comes to life — space is expanded.

Check with the nearest brick yard. You may find the makings of a number of things. Try using adobe flue liners for a sofa base or a coffee table. Space for stashing things away is an extra bonus. You never have too much storage space (25).

Make a place to "do your thing." A place to work at hobbies is one of the most important spots in a house. Most hobbies are messy; so plan an organized storage wall wherever you work. Try using discarded soft drink crates. They are great for keeping all the little junky things separated and in a place where you can easily find them. Use several, and add more as your accumulation multiplies — which is inevitable. Spray each crate with a different bright color to help you remember *what* you put *where*. Labels will help. Use plenty of pegboard for hanging small and large loseable tools.

Make a place to read and study. Once considered a status symbol, a desk is now a must; everyone needs a desk. It is an organizer for a kitchen, where it may be a simple wall-hung shelf to hold cookbooks, recipes, memos, and shopping lists. A drop-down front makes a counter for plan-

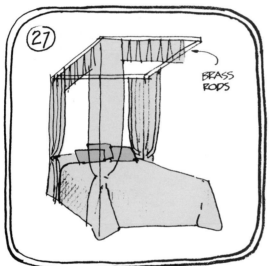

BRASS RODS

ning menus and paying bills while keeping an eye on the stove.

A table desk can go anywhere and will serve many purposes. Team it up with an inexpensive director's chair (26). And don't forget a desk for little people. Children love to play grownup by sitting at a desk to "study." Good study habits begin early and are encouraged here.

Enjoy decorating your bedroom. The key here is fabric. Instead of a headboard, run fabric up the wall and make a canopy. A brass rod on the ceiling is all that is necessary to support it (27). A bedroom is the most personal room in the house, and comfort is the main requirement. If you are doing a master bedroom, use restraint in your feminine inclinations. A man feels uncomfortable surrounded by lacy, frothy fabrics and pastel colors. Reserve these for a girl's room. Choose colors and textures that will create a room with a lived-in look. Avoid a delicate bedspread that says "stay off." Beds are to relax on, both at night and in the daytime. By anticipating how any household item will be used, much frustration can be prevented.

If you need a new shower stall, for little money you can get a fiberglass one. It goes into a 36-inch square corner, and fittings can be installed in either side. They are available in colors or in white. A curb keeps water from running out, and either curtains or a door may be added. An extra shower can add immeasurably to daily convenience. Shop and compare plumbing costs at your local stores.

In selecting appliances, look for those that are energy saving — hence,

(Upper left). Doing your own remodeling takes a minimum of know-how. Panels fit into place easily; then molding is nailed to the wall to provide support. (Upper right). The ceiling cross tees are snapped into place. (Left). The ceiling panels are laid into the grid formed by the cross tees. *Courtesy of Armstrong Cork Company.*

(Above). Combine the old and the new for chic decorating. Rough-hewn walls, vinyl floor, a gingham table cover, and a glistening table lamp make a charming setting for the early 18th-century chair. *Courtesy of Armstrong Cork Company.* (Upper right). Imagination created this multi-purpose room. Carpet tiles give comfort and gaiety. A painted oil drum makes a sturdy table base. A wired coolie hat becomes a lamp-shade. Cushions are covered with denim. *Courtesy of Armstrong Cork Company.*

money saving. Study the literature of the various manufacturers and the consumer bulletins. Look for appliances with low incidence of repair history — one of the best criteria of good quality.

A Formula for Successful Decoration

Decorating your own home successfully requires the application of this simple formula: *good taste applied to your own life-style and adapted to your personal budget.*

Acquire good taste through careful and conscientious study. Observe. Ask questions. Make a careful analysis of yourself and your family to be fully aware of your own life-style. Look closely at your financial resources and put them down on paper to see what you can comfortably afford. Straining the family budget beyond endurance is asking for trouble.

When you have done these things, you will be in a better position to decorate your own home than any outsider.

Experiment. If you make a mistake, correcting it may produce an unexpected delight. After you have become conscious of decorating skills, you will discover helpful hints on every hand. Start a file where you keep pictures of rooms, furniture, windows, floor plans, color schemes, and coordinated fabrics. Make notes of things you especially like in magazine pictures and in the homes of your friends. Have a space for questions, answered and unanswered.

Keep abreast of new materials and new trends, but be your own judge of what is right for you. The challenge to young Americans today is to create homes that are individually their own. Search for the best solutions to your particular problems. Welcome the help you can get from professional guidance, but make your home a product of your own creation. Only through a constantly rising level of taste and the ability to recognize and demand good and enduring design and values can you avoid mediocrity.

201

Suggestions and Assignments for Part 8: Stretching Your Dollar

Suggested Teaching Aids and Procedures

1. Stress the importance of acquiring the ability to see potential in discarded items.
2. Assign students to bring in their own creative ideas for budget decorating.
3. Discourage the use of too many knickknacks and artificial flowers.
4. Inform students that there are "how-to-do" kits on almost any home-making project. You may wish to locate some to demonstrate.

Student Assignments

1. Students should search through current periodicals for brochures, kits, and pamphlets on "how-to." *Woman's Day* and *Budget Decorating* are two excellent sources.
2. Other projects, left to the discretion of the teacher, depending upon the time allotted.

COLORPLATE 28. More color and more imagination! Flue tiles, small oil drums, wicker plates, a sturdy tile floor, and an inexpensive area rug skillfully combined create a room that can be the envy of some people who can afford much more. *Courtesy of Armstrong Cork Company.*

Looking to the Future

COLORPLATE 29. The lived-in
look. It is the accumulation of
"things" that makes a room a
haven. Much used and well-cared-
for wood becomes more beautiful
with age, and if the design is good,
it will always be in style. Live
your own way with the things that
are right for you. *Courtesy of
Ethan Allen.*

Decorating is an art, and, like any other art, if successful, is dependent upon a knowledge of design principles plus a genuine interest, a lot of patience, and personal dedication. In the eight categories below are listed some pertinent questions that will test your ability in the art of decoration. Most of the questions are answered in the text. For others you will find answers through further study and application of your own knowledge and skill. When you can answer these questions in the affirmative, you should feel confident to proceed with the ongoing process of making your house into a home with individuality and charm.

Test Your Talent for Decorating

Are Your Decisions Determined by Your Life-style?

1. When you think of planning a home, do you begin with yourself and whoever else will be sharing that home?

2. Do you consider the needs of your family — whether they be two or ten — more important than the approval of others?

3. Have you asked yourself and your family enough questions that you are fully aware of your own life-style?

4. Will you have the courage to base your decisions concerning your home on what is right for you, even if there are outside pressures to the contrary?

What About Arrangement and Organization of Space?

1. Do you recognize efficiently arranged space on a blueprint or in the floor plan of a house?

2. Would you have the courage to demand space where it is needed most, even if it meant foregoing frills that may impress your friends?

3. Can you arrange furniture in a given area for comfort and still make the room visually pleasant?

4. Can you arrange furniture in a small room to make it appear larger?

Can You Make Color Work for You?

1. Do you feel confident in the use of color?
2. Can you visualize your room with different colored walls, drapery, or furniture?
3. Can you apply the law of chromatic distribution in creating livable rooms?
4. Do you know what colors to choose to give a room a feeling of serenity? Or what colors to use to enliven a gloomy room?
5. What color would you choose as a background for an article to make it appear more conspicuous?
6. Can you judge from a small sample of paint or wallpaper what the effect will be when it covers all the walls in your room?
7. Do you know how to use color to alter the size and proportion of a room?
8. Can you bring balance into your room by means of color?
9. Will you have the courage to use the colors you enjoy living with in spite of current fads?

Have You Discovered the Magic of Fabric?

1. Regardless of numerous current magazine pictures to the contrary, can you be restrained in combining patterned fabrics? Do you have an eye for selecting fabrics with compatible scale, motifs, and colors in order to create rooms that can be lived in and enjoyed for a long time?
2. If you find, or have, a lovely fabric, can you use this as a basis for color-scheming your room?
3. Can you visualize ways in which fabric can solve your decorating problems?
4. Can you visualize a single window or an entire window wall taking on a completely new look through the use of a particular fabric?

How Practical Are You?

1. Are you realistic in choosing fabric with the right fiber for your particular purpose, even when another one is more appealing?
2. Would you select simple, sturdily built furniture for a family room in preference to lightweight ornate pieces?
3. Do you keep up on the latest in new materials in home furnishings but make sure all items have been sufficiently tried out before you make a purchase?
4. Will you choose a hard-wearing, dirt-hiding carpet for a heavily used area, even if you prefer the appearance of a much less practical one?
5. Do you avoid sacrificing functional lighting for a desire to create glamour?
6. Do you know where to economize and where to be extravagant?

Do You Recognize the Importance of Little Things?

1. Do you pay as much attention to the finishing touches of your room as you do to the big things?
2. Can you complete the little details to be consistent with the general character of the room?
3. Do you group small items to prevent clutter and eliminate knickknacks

that are neither beautiful, useful, nor meaningful to you?

Have You Cultivated Self-Discipline?

1. Do you keep your overall plan in mind whenever you make a purchase of *any* size?
2. Do you plan your shopping in advance and go equipped with tape measure, notes, and color swatches?
3. When you shop, do you keep in mind your specific needs and avoid being diverted by an eye-catching item or a persuasive salesperson?
4. Do you always keep before you the ultimate goal you wish to achieve?

How Perceptive Are You?

1. Can you distinguish good design of lasting merit from the faddish that may have an appeal for the moment only?
2. Do you recognize beauty in commonplace things?
3. Do you see true elegance in simplicity?

What Is An Interior Designer?

A frequent question most young people ask themselves is, "What do I want to do with my life?" "What would I like to spend my life doing?" "What am I best fitted for?" To those rare souls who know for certain from early youth what they want, life must be infinitely simplified. For most people, deciding on a career is a searching process. But a time comes when the decision must be made.

If you are creative, sensitive to your interior environment, interested in architecture, furniture, fabrics, and the decorative arts, you might want to examine the possibility of a career in interior design.

You may be wondering what has become of the "interior decorator." He is still around, but he functions under a different title. When decorating first became a profession, and for many years afterward, "interior decorator" was the accepted term for the person who decorated interiors. Today this term is seldom used since the connotation has come to be one who does merely a superficial embellishment of an interior. The term *interior design*, which implies the use of more comprehensive and professional skills, has been substituted for *interior decoration*, and the person who performs the necessary functions is no longer called an "interior decorator" but an "interior designer."

What are the Functions of an Interior Designer?

An interior designer is a trained expert who can convert ideas into reality. A designer starts with an idea and follows it through to completion, whether it be designing an entire building or one room. Often he or she works closely with the architect during the planning of the building. A designer is trained to visualize the completed room from the architectural background down to the last accessory. Much more is expected of the interior designer today than formerly. Successful interior decorating and design require knowledge, practice, and flair; and the trained professional can produce charming results with a surprisingly small budget.

A good designer will never impose his own tastes on the project. His true purpose is to interpret what the client wants and to execute it in such a way that *the final result reflects the personality of the client, not of himself.* This is the most difficult and yet the most subtle task of decorating, but it spells the difference between the amateur and the successful, experienced professional.

An important point the interior designer must keep in mind is the constant use of self-discipline in carrying through a job. Nearly always the temptation is to do too much. With the abundance of everything from which to choose, there is the danger of creating a feeling of ostentation. He should choose only those things which fit into the overall plan. A safe rule is to leave room for something to be added later. Too little is far safer than too much.

Before beginning the actual job, the designer's first task is to find out all he can about his client's life-style. What are her likes and dislikes? How do she and her family live? What are their interests, activities, and hobbies? How do they entertain? What are the particular quirks of family members that must be reckoned with? Does the client know what she wants, or will decisions be left up to the designer?

How much money can be spent? The better the designer knows his client and her family, the more successful the job will be.

The designer may be required to make a visual presentation of the project before it is begun (This is a skill that every designer must acquire). He then must make cost estimates for which he is held responsible. When the job has been agreed upon, the designer may take over the entire job of selecting colors, fabrics, furnishings, and accessories. He must find them, buy them, have them delivered, and install them. Or he may act as an adviser.

What Training is Necessary?

To be a practicing interior designer, one should have completed a program at an accredited college or university that offers a degree in interior design, or have earned a certificate of graduation from a reputable design school with an emphasis on interior design; he should then have a period of apprenticeship in a good interior design studio, furniture store, or department store during which time he works with an established designer. After this training period, he will find it advantageous to belong to one of the national organizations of professional designers.

Requirements for licensing interior designers are under study; in the near future a license will be required.

Career Opportunities in Interior Design

Upon completion of the training listed above, the student is prepared to take advantage of one or more of the following opportunities:

1. Entering a graduate program leading to professional opportunities in teaching (if he or she has earned a B. A. from an accredited college or university).
2. Becoming a member of a firm in which he or she will work with an architect in developing interiors.
3. Becoming a member of an interior design studio, in which he or she works directly with clients.
4. Working as a professional decorator-designer in a department store or a home furnishings store. Most such stores provide professional service.
5. Working as a professional renderer in a design studio.
6. Working as a professional designer in making interior setups for TV programs or for the theater.
7. Planning and arranging complete room setups for furniture companies for advertising purposes.
8. Writing newspaper articles on interior design.

These are only some of the employment opportunities open to the competent interior design student. The field of interior design is vast and is growing rapidly. In addition to furniture stores, department stores, and design studios, many other firms in related areas are finding a need for the trained designer. The student who adequately prepares himself for this profession will find opportunities in most areas throughout the country.

A Word to Young Marrieds

When you marry and begin to establish a home, you are in a business partnership — the most important one in which you will ever participate. Remember that a successful home is built on sound financing, and many aspects of it will be new to you. But if you enter it with a determination to make it succeed, the challenges you confront can be met with excitement and common sense. There will be real differences in personal preferences, requiring compromise in adapting the best ideas of each; but with mutual understanding and respect, the home you equip and run on a solid basis will be a constant source of enjoyment to you and to your future family. To accomplish this goal, the following guidelines may be useful:

1. Make all decisions together. You are now a family.
2. Live frankly and honestly within your resources. Make no apologies for what you do not have.
3. Do not try to begin with the kind of home that your parents have taken many years to establish. Begin with what you have now and plan for your future. You will be more likely to get what you want if you first know what you need.
4. Take time to think through and list the values you feel are most important. You are two people starting a life together. What do you want from life, and what are you willing to give? What are your values for life, and what is their order of priority? Write these values down and remember to read them regularly.
5. Make other lists. It is helpful to see things on paper. Make a list of "must-haves." These are the things that are essential, and you will find

that this list needn't be long. Make a list of "wants." These should be given priority according to your values and will likely take many years to acquire.

6. As you embark on the exciting project of decorating your first home, keep foremost in your mind your personal needs and your ideals for living. Grow together as you plan your home for work and for play, for intellectual and spiritual growth, for listening to music and dabbling in art, for working at whatever hobbies you like, and for just doing nothing.

7. As you begin your home, the numerous decisions may seem overwhelming. To avoid unnecessary frustrations, take your time. A home takes years in the making. Employ simple and logical solutions to the individual requirements of your overall plan. Avoid being swayed by some of the outlandish pictures in current magazines — often calling attention to the designer instead of illustrating livable rooms.

8. One of the challenges in today's living is finding enough space for your "things." Actually the solution is not always more space but organization of the space you have. For example, you can get twice as much into any given closet when it is efficiently organized. Decide what must go into an area; then plan the space accordingly. Storage room can be found in many unexpected places, such as on the back of a door, under the bed, or inside the barrel you made into a table.

9. Spend your money where you spend your time. If you sew, make a place for it. It needn't be a large place. A sewing corner as small as 7 feet by 2 1/2 feet will contain a counter to hold the machine. Put a pegboard above the counter to hold tape measure, shears, thread, plastic bags with zippers, lace, braid, and other necessary odds-'n'-ends. A small ironing board can fold down from the right side, and a tiny shelf will hold the iron. Everything you need will be there (1).

If you are a photography fan and like to finish your own pictures, a tiny closet can become a darkroom. Are you a builder or just a tinkerer? In either case, a corner of the garage, when organized, will contain all the "makings" and tools (2).

A well-planned kitchen, no matter how small, can be efficient. Make every inch count. The lack of space need not preclude a kitchen's being pleasant and cheerful. Make it pretty with the colors you like. While you do your daily tasks, feel like a queen, not like a drudge.

I f you are music lovers, make a place for stereo, records, and tapes.

10. Keep up-to-date with the explosive developments in all areas of home furnishing. Self-education is one of the most important responsibilities of today's homemaker. Let new technology help you. Let today's freedom help you in creating harmony out of what could be a hodgepodge. Give old treasures a new look. Let your design span the centuries by mixing today's geometrics with traditional curves and Early American with modern; use a Parsons table anywhere it works for you.

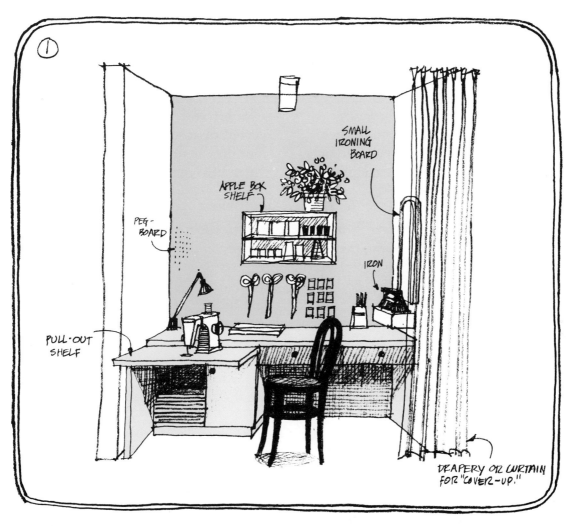

1

PEG-
BOARD

APPLE BOX
SHELF

SMALL
IRONING
BOARD

IRON

PULL-OUT
SHELF

DRAPERY OR CURTAIN
FOR "COVER-UP."

2

POP BOX

PEG BOARD

DOOR
HINGED TO
WALL

½ DOOR
HINGED TO WALL

213

11. Remember that a home is for people. It is a place to be lived in and used — a place for grownups to work, to enjoy their hobbies, to relax, or to entertain friends; a place for children with grimy hands, muddy shoes, peanut butter and jelly sandwiches, and pets. With today's technological developments in home furnishings, it is possible to have beauty and practicality at the same time. Now you can have your cake and eat it, too.

12. Wherever you live during the first years of your married life, you probably will dream of building a home of your own sometime. Hold fast to your dreams; they are the things out of which life is made.

In Your Dream Home

Make storage space for records from
Bach and Beethoven to Chopin and Dylan.
Reserve a shelf for
Shakespeare and Tolstoy, Wordsworth and Joyce.
Save wall space for
Da Vinci and Picasso to hang beside eventual children's "originals."
Arrange a comfortable spot for
intimate good talk about art, music, the theater, and politics.
Leave the door ajar for
friends to enter and share and add to the richness of your lives.

Bibliography

Allen, Phyllis Sloan. *Beginnings of Interior Environment.* Provo, Utah: BYU Press, 1972.

Bevlin, Majorie Elliott. *Design Through Discovery.* New York: Holt, Rinehart, and Winston, 1966.

Birren, Faber. *Principles of Color.* New York: Van Nostrand Reindhold Co., 1969.

Brostrom, Ethel, and Sloane, Louise. *Revive Your Rooms and Furniture.* New York: Bramhall House, n.d.

Cheskin, Louis. *Colors, What They Can Do for You.* New York: Leveright Publishing Corp., 1947.

Draper, Dorothy. *Decorating Is Fun.* Garden City, New York: Doubleday, 1962.

Evans, Ralph M. *An Introduction to Color.* New York: John Wiley and Sons, 1959.

Faulkner, Ray, and Faulkner, Sarah. *Inside Today's Home.* New York: Holt, Rinehart, and Winston, 1968.

Francis, Jo Ann, and Maco Publishing Co., eds. *The World of Budget Decorating.* New York: Simon and Schuster, 1967.

General Electric. *Light and Color.* Nela Park, Cleveland, Ohio: General Electric, 1968.

Gump, Richard. *Good Taste Costs No More.* New York: Doubleday, 1951.

How to Make Your Windows Beautiful. Kirsch: Sturgis, Michigan.

Larson, Leslie. *Lighting and Its Design.* New York: Whitney Library of Design, 1964.

Light for Living. American Home Lighting Institute, 360 North Michigan Avenue, Chicago, Illinois.

McCann, Karen Carlson. *Creative Home Decoration You Can Make: Low Cost Ways to Beautify Your Home.* Garden City, New York: Doubleday, 1968.

Reist, Janet Aston. *Elegant Decorating on a Limited Budget.* New York City: Macmillan Co., 1967.

St. Marie, Satenig S. *Homes are for People.* New York: John Wiley & Sons, 1973.

Listed below are a number of regular publications that should be of particular interest to today's young homemaker.

American Home. Downe Publishing, 641 Lexington Avenue, New York, New York 10022.

Apartment Living. Published six times yearly, Meredith Corporation, 1716 Locust Street, Des Moines, Iowa 50336.

Better Homes and Gardens. Published monthly, Meredith Corporation, 1716 Locust Street, Meredith

Budget Decorating. Published bimonthly, Maco Publishing Co., 635 Madison Avenue, New York, New York 10022.

Home Planning and Decorating. Published by Hudson Home Publications, 175 South San Antonio Road, Los Altos, California 94022.

1,001 Decorating Ideas. Published quarterly, Conso Publishing Co., 27 West 23rd Street, New York, New York 10010.

Women's Day Magazine. Published monthly,

Fawcett Printing Corporation, Louisville, Kentucky 40201.

Woverly's Easy to Do Decorating. Published semiannually by Pyramid Publications, A Division of Pyramid Communications, 919 Third Avenue, New York, New York 10022.

Some booklets on a variety of home decorating:

1,001 Decorating Ideas Home Library. A number of booklets on a variety of home furnishings subjects. 35c each. Conso Publishing Co., 635 Madison Avenue, New York, New York 10022.

Window Shade Manufacturers Association. 230 Park Avenue, New York, New York. Booklets on window shades. "Window Shade Primer" and "Do It Yourself Ideas for Window Shades."

Woman's Day Service Series. A how-to series on home decorating and repair. $1.25 each. Published by Fawcett Publications, Fawcett Building, Greenwich, Connecticut 06830.

Other readings:

All of the major manufacturers of fabrics, carpets, hard surface flooring, and furniture publish booklets that have valuable information on construction, design features, care, and use of their products. These may be had for a nominal fee or just for the asking.

For additional help, call the home demonstrator at your local city and county office. She is there to assist you and will have free booklets on many home decorating subjects.

Index

A

Accessories, 21-22, 190-92
    importance of, 208-9
Analogous color, 62
Apartments, 4
Architectural styles, 3-4
Art, grouping of, 44-45

B

Background color, 64-67
Books, 192-93
Bunk beds, 159

C

Canopy, making a, 198
Carpet materials, 86-87
Carpeting, 84-89
Carpets, cleaning of, 88-89
Color, 59-69
    effects on, 67-69
    make, work for you, 208
Color wheel, 59-60
Complementary color, 62
Condominium, the, 4-6
Conversation area, 34-39
Creative accessories, 194-96
Curtains and drapes, 101-6
    estimating yardage for, 124-26
    how to make, 135-39
    materials for, 101-6
    selecting fabric for, 126-28

D

Denim, 188
Design
    decorative, 22-23
    structural, 22
Design principles, xviii
    and decorating, 207

E

Elements of design, 29-32
    color as an, 30
    form as an, 30
    light as an, 30-33
    line as an, 29-30
    pattern as an, 29
    space as an, 30
    texture as an, 29
Environment, in the home, xiii
    importance of, xvii-xviii

F

Fabrics, 106-9
    magic of, 208
    to rejuvenate a room, 187-90
    solving problems with, 106

Factory-built home, the, 7-10
Fashion in home furnishings, 22
Floor plan, basic requirements of a, 12-13
Flooring, 79-84
    chart, 80-83
Flowers and plants, 193-94
Furnishings, buying, 147-61
Furniture
    arranging, 33-40
    bargains in, 172-73
    construction of, 148-50
    design of, 148
    first aid for, 163
    flexibility of, 148
    making your own, 173-81
    marketing terms for, 155-56
    multipurpose, 171-72
    refinishing, 181-84
    selection of, 156-60
    upholstered, tips for buying, 155
Furniture care, 163
Furniture purchases, a survey report of, 160-63

G

Golden mean, 24
Good taste, achieving, 21-47

H

Hobbies, a place for, 196

Home, xvii-xviii
    choices of, 3-10
Hues, of color, 61

I

Intensity, 61
Interior designer, 209-11

M

Mobile home, 6-7
Monochromatic color, 62

N

Neutralization of color, 61-62

P

Painting, 184-87
Paints, kinds of, 184-87
Patterns, and combining fabrics, 108-9
Perception, 209
Piano, placing the, 39
Picture hanging, 43-45
Plan of a house, 11-13
Plastic in furniture, 152-55
Polyfoam furniture, 158-59

Principles of design, 23-28
    balance as a, 24-26
    emphasis as a, 26
    harmony as a, 26-29
    proportion as a, 24
    rhythm as a, 26
    scale as a, 23-24

S

Seating, 35-36
Self-discipline, 209
Sheets, 188
Shower stall, installing a, 198-201
Small room, problems of a, 40-43
Space, 11-12
    arrangement and organization of, 207-8
Stackable furniture, 159
Study area, creating a, 196-98
Suitability of decorating, xviii

T

Tables, function of, 40
Towels, 188

V

Value, of color, 61
Values, xiii

W

Wall coverings, 89-95
    chart, 90-91
Wallpaper, 90-95
Walls, 43-45
Window hangings, types of, 122-24
Window terminology, 118-22
Windows, 117-39
    types of, 117-18
Wood paneling, 89-90

Y

Yardage, estimating, for curtains
    or drapes, 124-26
Young marrieds, as a market in home
    furnishings, xiii-xiv